JOHN ARMSTRONG was until recently Philosopher in Residence at the Melbourne Business School and is Senior Adviser to the Vice-Chancellor of Melbourne University. He is the author of several internationally acclaimed books on art, aesthetics and philosophy, the latest of which, *In Search of Civilization*, was published in 2009.

THE SCHOOL OF LIFE is dedicated to exploring life's big questions: *How can we fulfil our potential? Can work be inspiring? Why does community matter? Can relationships last a lifetime?* We don't have all the answers, but we will direct you towards a variety of useful ideas – from philosophy to literature, psychology to the visual arts – that are guaranteed to stimulate, provoke, nourish and console.

# How to Worry
# Less about Money
John Armstrong

MACMILLAN

First published 2012 by Macmillan
an imprint of Pan Macmillan, a division
of Macmillan Publishers Limited

Pan Macmillan
20 New Wharf Road, London N1 9RR
Basingstoke and Oxford
Associated companies throughout the world
www.panmacmillan.com

ISBN 978-1-4472-0229-5

The picture acknowledgements on p.149
constitute an extension of this copyright page.

Case studies, except where the author is
the subject of them, have been fictionalized
and have had names changed to protect the
identities of the people concerned.

9 8 7

A CIP catalogue record for this book is
available from the British Library.

Cover design by Marcia Mihotich
Design and setting by seagulls.net
Printed and bound by CPI Group (UK) Ltd,
Croydon, CR0 4YY

Visit www.panmacmillan.com to read
more about all our books and to buy
them. You will also find features,
author interviews and news of any
author events, and you can sign up for
e-newsletters so that you're always first
to hear about our new releases.

# Contents

# I. Introduction

This book is about worries. It's not about money troubles. There's a crucial difference.

Troubles are urgent. They ask for direct action. *I don't see how I can meet my car-insurance bill. I never pay down my credit-card debt: it is like a millstone round my neck. I really wish I could send my fourteen-year-old to a private school because he is floundering where he is. But I cannot afford it.*

Money troubles like these can be met in only two ways. *Either* you gain access to more money – by adjusting debts, earning more or cutting costs. *Or* you go without something else.

By contrast, worries often say more about the worrier than about the world.

Worries are about what is going on in your head, not just what is going on in your bank account. They range freely over time: *I worry that I made a terrible financial decision fifteen years ago. I worry that my children, when they are adults, will not have enough money.* Worries are connected to imagination and the emotions, not just to what is happening here and now.

So, addressing money *worries* should be quite different from dealing with money *troubles*. To address our worries we have to give attention to the pattern of thinking (ideology) and to the scheme of values (culture) as these are played out in our own individual, private existences.

*

Typically, advice about money addresses the question: *how can I get more money?* The advice consists of suggestions and instructions for increasing one's wealth: develop a property portfolio; get a better paying job; marry someone rich. It assumes that we already know how much we need ('More! more!') and why ('Are you crazy?'). Yet the question 'how can I get more money?' should, ideally, be asked only after enquiry into how much money I need and what I need it for.

Alternatively, money advice asks: *how can I get by with less?* There are many money-saving ideas: cut up your credit card; force yourself to record all expenditure; turn the heating down and wear an extra jumper at home; collect special-discount coupons. These could be very useful strategies, obviously. It assumes that you have already set the right goals and just want to get there with less expense. But they don't address the underlying question: *what do I properly need money for?* Or to put it another way: *what's the link between money and the good life?*

In other words, our culture of advice is attuned to money *troubles*, rather than money *worries*. This is a problem because the theme of money is so deep and pervasive in our lives. One's relationship with money is lifelong, it colours one's sense of identity, it shapes one's attitude to other people, it connects and splits generations; money is the arena in which greed and generosity are played out, in which wisdom is exercised and folly committed. Freedom, desire, power, status, work, possession: these huge ideas that rule life are enacted, almost always, in and around money.

In the philosophy of teaching, a big distinction is made between training and education. Training teaches a person how to carry out a specific task more efficiently and reliably. Education, on the other hand, opens and enriches the person's mind. To train a person, you need know nothing about who they really are, or what they love, or why. Education reaches out to embrace the whole person. Historically, we have treated money as a matter for training, rather than education in its wider and more dignified sense.

How one relates to money is framed, ultimately, by one's most extensive and least explicit ideas – ideas about the human condition, 'the meaning of life, the universe and everything'. And this means that one's relationship with money can be helped or hindered by apparently quite distant thoughts.

For instance, Karl Marx argued that money is part of a system that is profoundly unjust. It damages both those who succeed and those who have an obviously hard time. Escape might be possible – but only by rejecting the system as a whole, by stepping off the conveyor belt, by revolution. Money, framed this way, feels like an alien imposition on the world.

The free-market advocates of the Chicago School, on the other hand, argued that money is essentially a neutral medium, through which people interact rationally in order to maximize their own utility. Framed this way, money is harmless. Any failings that may seem to be due to money are in fact the product of failures of rationality. A person's economic life is a free creation.

These are big intellectual constructs and surely few people go around with such precise and elaborate models of money in their heads. But we do go around with some sort of model – more vague, more poetic, more humdrum, as it may be. We bring a vision of life and the world to our interaction with money. The point isn't to immediately agree or disagree with Marx or the free-market theorists. Rather, their viewpoints can be prompts to a more personal task: what, really, is my (or your) equivalent theory of money? And this question points to a major ambition of this book: to help us come to our own big views about money and its role in life.

# II.  Thinking about Money

# 1. What are Money Worries Really About?

Worries about money tend to fall into four big groups:

1. *Without it my life is going to have lots of pains and hassles.* I'll be humiliated because I do not have enough money to protect myself. I will have low status.

2. *Money will force me to spend a lot of my life just making enough to get by.* This is not a complete waste; it's just that there will be a lot less fulfilment, self-realization and worthwhile endeavour than I'd like. I'll pass a lot of my life thinking about debt payments and credit cards – rather than dealing with ultimately more important matters. What's more, money is extremely unreliable. I'll save, and then it will all disappear away because of some gyration of the market.

3. *I'll miss out on the good things that I long for.* I'll never live in a lovely house, drive an elegant car, go on a fabulous holiday, feel the snug warmth and ease that I assume derives from deep financial security. And this makes me angry with myself and with the world. I worry that I will fail in life and this will be connected to my inability to deal better with money.

4. *Money is like a virus.* For the sake of money people do terrible things. Money seems to operate with a logic that is indifferent to merit or suffering or justice. There is a kind of fate that, for no good reason, determines that *this* person will scrape and beg while *that* person will gaze at statements from stockbrokers filled with huge numbers. The system feels too big – there is nothing I, or anyone, can do about it.

If we are to do something about our worries we need to understand them before trying to immediately respond to them. Where do our worries come from? What lies behind them? What are we really worried about? We make progress in our lives when we turn anxieties into specific questions. Providing, that is, we turn them into the right questions.

Money *worries* occur because we cannot give accurate enough answers to the underlying questions:

1. What do I need money for? That is, what is important to me?
2. How much money do I need to do that?
3. What is the best way for me to get that money?
4. What are my economic responsibilities to other people?

These questions engage directly with the worries with which we started. The questions are serious but they have real answers.

Our natural tendency is to spin from one worry to another; we change topic, as it were, but do not really get anywhere:

A more desirable habit of thinking is one in which worries are held in the mind, so that they can be turned into genuine enquiries:

WORRIES  ➡  QUESTIONS  ➡  ANSWERS

It might sound a touch pedantic to emphasize this. But it is a crucial principle. We will never make progress in addressing our money worries if we do not recognize that they stem from a set of underlying questions. And those questions are about our own values, mode of living and view of life. Our worries – when it comes to money – are about psychology as much as economics, the soul as much as the bank balance.

So the first task is to know our worries and to trace them back to an underlying question. It's quite possible that, on a first examination, the worries are a bit vague. I often don't really know what I am really worried about. That's not to say that my distress has no cause. It's just that I don't know very accurately what the cause is.

For instance, I quite often feel anxious about money when I look at my car. I've had it for ten years and it has accumulated quite a number of scratches and minor ailments. It creaks in a curious way; the wipers shudder across the windscreen; the bits of plastic that protected the underside of the wheel arches fell off some time back. The interior never feels entirely clean. There's a dent on one side caused by some ill-judged reversing in an underground car park. But it goes and is reliable. And I can't afford to replace it.

But some part of my brain tells me that it is not the car I am supposed to have. I imagine something more interesting, or more beautiful – or just more up-market. When I park at the tennis club I feel relieved if there are other modest cars around and (I'm ashamed to say, but it is true) annoyed by the sight of more elegant vehicles.

Looking at my car makes me worry about money – but what is the source of the anxiety?

What causes my anxiety is the thought that I am stuck with this thing, that I'll never get anything better: I'll never be able to afford to be happy about my car.

This worry, it turns out, is not really to do with the car itself. Rather, it is to do with imagination and social relations. So, what exactly am I worrying about? On reflection, it emerges that I'm worried about not taking care of things properly. If I'd looked after the car properly, it could still be in fine condition. Then I wouldn't worry about it being ten years old and an average make. When I look at the car, I'm seeing (I now understand) the consequence of a kind of laziness – always putting off getting little things fixed, never cleaning the back seats, etc. My worry is about my character. And buying a new car – which would be a real burden – would not make me better at looking after it. In fact, I think the appeal of a new car is really to do with starting over: next time, I secretly tell myself, I'll take good care of my vehicle. But that's delusional. I didn't in the past. Why would that change now?

It's really quite significant that the 'object' of the worry may be far from clear. It means, as I have said, that the primary task is to think, rather than rush to a solution.

To take another example: anxiety arises, for me, in connection with a specific grand hotel in Venice. When I think about it – it's extremely elegant and charming and wildly expensive – I feel frustrated and despondent. I contemplate my meagre bank account with disgust. I'll never be able to stay there. Of course, there are millions of things I can't begin to afford, millions of high-price hotels. Why the worry about this specific hotel?

Thinking it through, I realize – for the first time – that I associate that hotel with historical figures I admire. I think John Ruskin stayed there. I'm pretty sure the writer Cyril Connolly did, and the historian Kenneth Clark. To me the hotel means: you can be like them. Although, the thought looks silly once it is presented to daylight. Staying there would do nothing at all to make me similar to them in any important way. But this suggests that the worry is not ultimately about money. It is, ultimately, a worry that, in comparison with these men I admire, I am unfocused and short on courage. These are concerns worth addressing; but a luxury hotel isn't the answer.

Another money worry is that when my children grow up they will not make enough money. I try to devise ways of saving now so that they will be secure. If I put a small amount aside every week, what will compound interest make of it in fifty years time? (Admittedly rather too far off to be much help.) But the real worries, I now think, are of their inner independence and of the radically indefinite character of the future. Maybe they won't care about what seems important to me. I'm confronting the fact that I can't imagine them grown up. How could the little girl playing in the sandpit earn a middle-class income? The worry, then, is existential: my children will grow up, they will become their own judges of life; they will separate from me.

We often don't quite know what the problem is that we need a solution to. My worries, here, are clearly only in part about money. They are also worries about being liked, about the well-being of my children, about my relationship with my secret hopes of fulfilment and achievement, and about the coherence of my life. But of course these are quite vague starting points. The temptation is to say that because they are vague they can be dismissed. In fact, it is *because* they are vague that they require extra attention and clarification.

# 2. A Good Relationship with Money

One thing that's characteristic of a good relationship is this: you get more accurate at assigning responsibility. When things go wrong you can see how much is your fault and how much is the fault of the other person. And the same holds when things go well. You know that part of it is your doing and part depends on the contribution of your partner.

This model applies to money. When things go well or badly, it's partly about what you bring to the situation and partly about what money brings. What money brings is a certain level of spending power.

What you bring to this relationship includes imagination, values, emotions, attitudes, ambitions, fears and memories. So the relationship is absolutely not just a matter of pure economic facts of how much you get and how much you spend.

The relationship model suggests that fixing issues around quantity, or how much money you have, very often won't, on its own, make the difference one is looking for. That is, trying to solve all your money worries by addressing the *quantity* of money – either by increasing it or managing with less – isn't the ideal strategy. What is key is addressing your relationship with money and the feelings you have about it.

They contemplate the mystery of existence – money feels irrelevant.
Caspar David Friedrich, *Moon Rising over the Sea*, 1822.

She contemplates the mystery of existence – money feels central and overwhelming.

The conflicts between the concerns of money and the hopes of life are real and deep. There are times when we think they might line up – when money might dovetail with happiness. There are other points at which the opposition seems really painful. A big electricity bill comes in and the house-insurance payment is due and I need expensive dental treatment. I can barely manage. And it always seems to be like this. Will I never be able to visit my sister overseas? Will we never be able to install the new kitchen that would really improve our family life?

It's important to recognize the grandeur of the theme of money in individual and collective life. Our struggles around money are akin to some of the great moral dramas of the past – dramas that tend to have more prestige in our cultural imaginings than the conflicts of day-to-day life. Take, for instance, the fight between faith and reason, or the potential clash of individual needs and the demands of the state.

In Sophocles' *Antigone* there is an elemental clash between private life and the duty to society. The central character, Antigone, puts her loyalty to her brother – who is a traitor – above her loyalty to the city where she lives. Is she right to do so, even when the city is in grave danger?

The grandeur of the play comes from the fact that, as spectators, we can see the justice and reasonableness of both sides of the argument. A tragic conflict is being presented. We can feel the power and propriety of each claim.

Similarly, the claims of money and of life can feel as if they are involved in a struggle to the death. You might grow up (as I did) in a grim environment and long to make enough money to escape it. But that can feel like losing your roots. Or, in order to make enough money to survive in a competitive world, you might feel you have to sell out and never devote yourself to the things that you wish you could focus on, like family, creativity, changing the world or simply cultivating your garden.

We have to try to reach some kind of accommodation – some kind of proper understanding of the relationship between, and integration of, these opposed demands. So that there can be a non-tragic resolution. We miss the point of the play if we simply side with Antigone; just as we misunderstand the theme of money if we simply say money is terrible. It is (in some ways) terrible, but it is also (potentially) very good.

With *Antigone*, Sophocles was showing his contemporaries the depth and power of certain conflicts. The tensions, uncertainties and confusions in one's relationship with money are great themes in life, not distractions from it. Probing our disappointments, making tough decisions about priorities, becoming independent, surviving hardship, putting off a short-term pleasure for a long-term benefit: these are crucial aspects of mature living, not just unfortunate detours imposed by money.

Angst is unavoidable. Money is such an important theme in life that we *should* worry about it. The goal is not to avoid *all* anxious or sobering thoughts about money. (Although a business friend of mine *says* that's exactly what he wants: 'I'd love to never think about money again; another couple of million and I won't have to.')

We shouldn't avoid the painful, uncertain and difficult aspects of our individual and collective relationships with wealth and poverty.

Worry is a name for mental effort: ideally one wants to worry more insightfully and more purposefully. The aim of adult life, one might say, is to worry well. We worry about things that matter; worry implies care. So: how *much* should you care about money? In what ways should you care about money? And for what reasons should you care about money? Should you feel fearful of money? Self-knowledge, skill and courage – the true antidotes to fear – do not make danger go away. They enable us to live a more flourishing life, *despite* the existence of danger.

A courageous person isn't one who simply fails to notice a threat. They are acutely aware of the risks; it's just that, instead of being paralysed or intimidated, they are determined and confident enough to face those risks.

So, as individuals we have the opportunity to change what we bring to our relationship with money. We're not trying to be *indifferent* to it; rather, we want a wise relationship with it. That's what this book is about – how we can bring imagination, self-knowledge, emotional maturity, and our big ideas about life and society, into the way we engage with money.

# III.  The Secret Meaning of Money

# 1. When Money is Not Money

Emotional baggage, hang-ups and obsessions can cause problems in all kinds of relationships. So it is only natural that these are sources of trouble in one's relationship with money as well. And we don't necessarily realize what money means to our deep imaginations. It might mean status, security, success, revenge, salvation, moral superiority or guilt (to start the list). These are all huge themes in life that get caught up with and played out in our relationship with money – and sometimes this happens in unfortunate ways.

To see such entanglements close up, consider these intimate portraits of people I know.

## i. Eddie

For years Eddie used to say that a bit more money would much improve his relationship with his wife. His idea was that if they could afford to go out to dinner once a week, and pay for a babysitter, he and his wife would get to have proper conversations, and thus intrigue and excite one another. And they'd have excellent sex. Over the years they've made enough money to afford some evenings out. But they don't do it.

The problem wasn't and isn't just about money – although Eddie keeps insisting that it is. Recently he was saying that, if they could move to a bigger and considerably more expensive house, *then* they'd feel great about each other, they'd relish going out to dinner and their marriage would heat up.

For Eddie, money has a *secret meaning*. It is the magical solver of relationship woes. In his head, money is a kind of aphrodisiac. This false equation derives from quite a specific experience to do with his parents. When he was a child, Eddie used to hate it when his parents went out to dinner. Once, when his mother was all dressed up to go out, he was actually sick on her shoes because he was so hysterical at the thought of being left with the babysitter while his parents enjoyed themselves without him. Also, when he was a child, his mother getting 'all dressed up to go out' represented 'lots of money'. The connection struck deep into his imagination: money equals adults having an enviable time together. So now, when his marriage is not exciting enough, it feels to him as if the solution must be *more money*.

This means that money is being asked to do something impossible. Eddie wants a money solution to a romantic problem. He doesn't see this. It's true that relationship problems are quite often caused by money. You get stressed because you carry more debt than you can manage (debt, in fact, ruined Eddie's parents' marriage). You both become edgy and worried. You fight. More money would help the relationship, you tell yourself, because the problem is, at root, a money problem.

So we are used to the idea that money can ease relationship tensions. Only that's not what's going on in Eddie's case. He has, first and foremost, a relationship problem, but he experiences it as money trouble.

## ii. James

Over the last three decades James has built up a substantial fortune through his property ventures and various other businesses. He's among the thousand richest UK citizens. He is terrified of failure and poverty.

His wealth is actually pretty secure. He owns land, buildings, cars, horses, furniture. He has a conservative investment portfolio. He's put money in various trusts for his family. He holds many insurance policies. He has largely moved out of the businesses he started, so he doesn't now carry those risks. His fear is irrational. But obviously that doesn't stop it being emotionally powerful.

Because James feels that he's got money trouble. He honestly feels he has not got enough. He looks at the statements of his assets and he is filled with anxiety. More is urgently needed.

The real solution to his worries cannot possibly be economic. If a small castle in Scotland, a mansion in the Lake District, a house in Edinburgh's New Town and all those shares and policies and trusts do not make him feel secure then – one may safely assume – nothing of that kind could. His worry is not really economic at all. It just feels economic.

The consoling of his terror needs to be pursued along more hopeful lines. Perhaps art or religion or a change in his attitude to his family could make a difference. But because James feels that his worries are about money, he does not turn his hungry intelligence in those other directions.

In James's imagination, money is like an unreliable mother – liable at any moment to abandon her child. While he feels this way he cannot effectively use money to calm his fears. Hence, no matter how much money he accumulates, his anxieties do not diminish.

In other words, James is caught in a trap. Half of his brain insists that money will make him feel safe; the other half insists that money is unreliable. So no matter how much he accumulates, the level of anxiety is not reduced.

In order to have a better relationship with money, James will have to do something that looks, at first sight, irrelevant to his economic life. He will have to confront the inner demons of his insecurity.

## iii. Petra

For as long as she can remember, Petra has felt locked into intense rivalry with her cousin Simone. Although they have barely spoken in the last five years, Petra has a private scale of comparison by which she judges her own life. When she hears, from mutual acquaintances, of Simone's increasing professional success, Petra gets quite disturbed. It's partly because, for a number of years, she was better off than Simone. When Simone went back to law school, Petra was the affluent one: she had the nice place to live, she went on the big holidays. Deep down, Petra unconsciously formed the belief that her superior affluence was proof that she was superior to Simone in other ways: more intelligent, friendlier, nicer, more attuned to reality, more deserving of a good life.

Petra's attitude to money puzzles her friends. She is a fairly senior civil servant, on a salary three times the national average. She is single, with a son now aged twenty. But Petra often contemplates her own lot with disgust. She hates her apartment (though her friends admire the way she has arranged it). She feels a failure. She's always dreaming of what she would do *if only she had more money.*

In Petra's imagination, money is the territory in which she competes with her cousin. How much money does she need? 'More than Simone' is, secretly, the only answer bearable to her.

## iv. Angela

If ever Angela finds herself a bit ahead financially, it doesn't last.

A couple of years ago her father's aunt died and left Angela about £20,000. It's all gone. She went on a trip to Italy. She lost some of it to a stupid Kangaroo-farming investment scam. She gave 10 per cent to a women's refuge. She took a lot of taxis for a while. She tried a bit of psychotherapy, but it didn't do much for her. She bought a beautiful little early-eighteenth-century walnut side table – it's out of place in the shared house she rents, but it's the one lasting thing she's got from the inheritance.

When she's feeling pinched and burdened, Angela looks back with horror at the melting away of that lump sum. Why didn't she just put it in the bank?

She feels frustrated with work. She can't seem to find a job she really likes. She day dreams about working for a fascinating consultancy firm she's heard of, based in Copenhagen; they work in business philosophy and it sounds to her like a fusion of Andy Warhol's Factory and the Boston Consulting Group. But it feels hopelessly distant as a career option. She's doing a part-time Masters in Applied Ethics – and, to be honest, it's not going very well. She has a job she used to like: teaching people to teach English as a foreign language.

Strange though it sounds, Angela is afraid of having enough money. She says she wants to earn more and save more; she is sick of always being in debt. In her imagination money is very dangerous. She's 34, but managing herself financially equals the death of her youth and the onset – so she thinks – of bleak middle age. She feels that she has money worries. Behind them, however, lie unexpected causes – her attitude to herself and her life; her vision of ageing and maturity; her private theories of happiness.

## v. Stephen

Stephen thinks of himself as poor. He often uses the word 'struggling' in the private dialogues in which he talks through his worries with himself. He works in a bookshop. When he can, he works on his own writing: he's been trying to get a collection of short stories published, so far without success. He is utterly painstaking and serious about literary creation – he tries to capture tiny movements of feeling with total fidelity; he experiments with new and difficult forms of presentation. He is horrified when he looks at the titles that sell well. There's so much dross and cheap, easy stuff that makes millions. Money, he feels, is the enemy of truth and substance. Money crushes anyone who tries to stand in its way. It erects false standards. In his head, publishers don't care how good a piece of writing is, they only care how much profit they can make from it. At parties, if he says he's a writer people only care about how many copies he sells. He compares the flat he rents in a run-down street with the big, vulgar houses in wealthier streets. He walks past shops filled with fake luxuries and objects that are only about status, and branded goods that steal people's souls. We live, he says, in Plato's cave. Everyone is obsessed with things that are not real – with money rather than truth. And when he tries to point this out, of course, they hate him.

## vi. Karen

In the last few years, after her children started school, Karen has established a second career as a financial planner; before that, she was a sports teacher. Her work brings her into close contact with people who have a lot more money than her. She's become acutely conscious of the links between money and status. Obviously, the more money a client has the more important they are to her business and the more care and attention are devoted to them. When, in the social pages of a glossy magazine, she sees a photograph of one or other of her clients at a charity event or at the races she knows the back-story. She knows how wealth creates presence: who is friends with whom; how the varied strata of 'society' are differentiated. She can usually tell very quickly whether a person has real wealth or is just 'aspirational' (a term of abuse in her private vocabulary). In some ways she is excited by these close encounters with the rich. But they have also made her rather steely. She's unconsciously impatient with, and bored by, her old non-affluent friends. And she is completely determined to find a way of getting herself up there in what looks like the real world – the world of wealth.

The growing internal pressure around money that Karen feels has nothing to do with having enough to get by. Money means status – that is: love, attention, respect, pride in oneself, fullness of being. In other words, money has taken on an almost religious significance for her. It, for her, is what an earlier society might have called 'the grace of God'. So a genuine solution to her troubles might look very little like a financial strategy and a lot more like moral regeneration.

These portraits are just a few examples of the fact that, deep down, very often *money is not money*. It is proof of goodness; it is the cause of evil; it is victory over a rival; it is the path to love; it is guarantor of sexual pleasure; it is poison; it is the death of childhood.

Because money is so pervasive in our lives it is inevitable that it gets entangled with intimate psychology. For a novelist that may be exciting. In terms of living well it's a problem.

It's a problem because, to allow, for instance, my relationship with my parents to invade my savings account, or to try to gain belated victory in a childhood rivalry by maximizing my mid-life earnings, will only result in failure. These past experiences should not influence my monetary decisions today.

Strictly speaking, money is just a neutral mechanism for exchange. It isn't anything in itself. It merely records a degree of debt or credit. But from a psychological point of view, money – as we have been seeing – is a lot of different things. At one extreme, someone might regard money as a kind of god. This is not a matter of explicit belief. Rather, it is revealed in how a person thinks and feels and acts. Or, at another extreme, someone might act as if money is evil, and therefore they feel impelled to fail economically, and derive from that failure some degree of validation. But – of course – the price of that validation is extremely high.

Money exerts a strange power and causes us to behave in unfortunate ways.

We tend to tell ourselves lies about money. The secret meaning of money in our individual imaginations provides a powerful motive for avoiding or embroidering the truth: for lying. Economics makes itself a science by excising the personal, but it thereby misses what we most need to understand: the secret history of our individual relationships to money.

A lot of people feel they have no business thinking about money *in general*. The particularities of their experience are too odd and too personal. How can one speak authentically and with any general relevance? *Who am I to speak about money?* the voice of self-criticism asks.

What we must do, therefore, is strip off these layers of doubt and confusion; we need to see money as realistically as possible. For our own well-being and for the good of society we should attempt to reform and improve our relationships to money. We want to cast off the unhelpful baggage. But how do we do this?

# 2. How to Strip Off

This is a practical, four-step exercise in self-knowledge. It's worth actually writing down (as honestly as possible) your own answers.

## i. Acknowledgement

Because the secret meaning that money has in one's own life is always a bit hidden, it's easy to deny that meaning. One's instinctive reaction can be to say, 'Of course, other people carry all kinds of baggage about money – I, however, am completely free from such impediments.' Start by resisting this tendency. The process begins when you say, 'I probably treat money in some strange ways – only I don't yet know exactly what these ways are.'

## ii. Associations

Start with some words or phrases you associate with money. To embolden your list-making, here are some of mine (some of which I admit look a bit strange at first): Hassles, 'I'll never escape', 'The sunlit uplands', Vulgarity, Snug, 'It's OK for *you*'.

Then flesh out what's going on. What do these words or phrases mean to you? Add a reflection on what they reveal about your attitude to money. Here are mine:

1. *Hassles*: having to live in a really inconvenient place (because property is more affordable there), *hence* a long commute, *hence* being frantic in the morning, *hence* being irritable and brusque with Helen and the children, *hence* feeling guilty and sad. *Reflection*: my fear of taking proper responsibility for my own time-management links up with not having the ideal amount of money. But the hassles are exaggerated – I should get up earlier, which means going to bed earlier, which means switching off the DVD and not watching just one more episode of *The West Wing*.

2. *'I'll never escape'*: this is a fatalistic feeling. Whenever I've got a bit of money in hand there always comes a big bill or expense that I hadn't allowed for. This always takes up all the money I thought I had saved. I'm just feeling a little bit smug, and then Helen says that the dental bill for the children's braces has to be paid, or a bit of the roof is going to have to be replaced. Back to zero. *Reflection*: the problem is I bury my head in the sand. I need to anticipate more realistically. I've known for ages that the braces would cost quite a lot; we knew that bit of the roof was in a bad way. But part of me just ignored this.

3.  *'The sunlit uplands'*: code for – 'One day all will be well.' I often fantasize about having more money. I imagine how lovely that would be – all my troubles would be over, I'd have a great time. But there is no timeline. 'One day' is just some indefinite time far into the future. *Reflection*: I think of money in a slightly magical way. I don't think realistically about *how* I could make this happen, even if only to a limited degree.

4.  *Vulgarity*: I'm always on the lookout for signs that people with a lot of money are inferior to me in some way that I prize. I'm obsessed with beauty and I feel better about myself when I see well-off people who are brash and gaudy. *Reflection*: I'm trying to hold on to my dignity in the face of uncomfortable economic comparisons. I could do that better by concentrating on what I care about and not bothering so much about criticizing others.

5.  *Snug*: my image of what money would bring. A cashmere coat, on a cold evening; thick velvet curtains, perfectly fitted; inner tranquillity born of not having to worry about money. *Reflection*: this idea about money seems to be related to my Scottish childhood – it is a defence against feeling cold. Maybe it is to do with protection against other dangers. If I have money, no-one will get angry with me. When I'm honest, I know money can't bring that kind of safety.

6. *'It's OK for you'*: I might say this about another person; and I fear another person might say it about me. I imagine it being said in a very bitter, resentful tone of voice. It says: I'm unhappy because you are happy. And implies: I will be happy when you are unhappy. *Reflection*: I don't think I am actually bitter. But I'm terrified that I could become so. And I'm afraid of other people feeling bitter towards me. Has my obsession with improving my own lot made me a bit selfish?

## iii. Private History

To cultivate self-awareness you need to examine the key episodes of your private money history. Are you proud of yourself in relation to money? When have you been most humiliated or embarrassed about money? How did you feel about the people who were around at that time? How has money figured in your relationships? Did your upbringing encourage a healthy attitude towards money?

To what extent do you attribute 'magical' powers to money? Do you pay more attention to how much money people *seem* to have or to the more delicate question of how much they *actually* have? Have your worries, in retrospect, been wise? Have you been over optimistic? What are your real fears about money?

In order to encourage you, and get you going, here are some chapters from my own secret history with money:

1. Aged 7, telling the wild lie that my father was 'almost a millionaire' (actually he was enjoying a mildly affluent episode in an epic of profit and loss) and instantly being cut down: 'You are such a moron.' *Fear*: I am boastful. I am drawn to ridiculous exaggeration of my economic status because I am terrified of being humiliated. I unconsciously equate wealth with desirability. Yet I know that to do so is absurd.

2. My parents' terrifying veering between the marks of sophisticated wealth (antique crystal decanters, holidays in Provence, camelhair coats) and real poverty (a bashed-up little car that once broke down in the main street; their inability to buy food or pay for the heating in winter; the holes in my shoes – and my reluctance to ask my parents to pay for new ones). *Fear*: I can't accept the reality of money; I see it as a stage-prop; it comes and goes for no reason connected to my behaviour or decisions; I hold myself absolved of responsibility. It is out of my hands.

3. My sweet-natured young sister, then aged 12, after we had paid a call on a wealthy local family, getting into the car and gasping 'They're so rich!' and my mother, brother and I hissing at her to shut up – though only we could conceivably have heard her. Why were we so angry? *Fear*:

my vanity is wounded by the idea of poverty; I can't bear to be reminded of it.

4.  Being humiliated by my first girlfriend, who came from an over-achieving family. She felt short of money though she was hugely privileged by my standards. She explained her parents' attitudes towards me: 'They like you, but you are a mystery to them; they think young men should buy sports cars and set up publishing companies or get into parliament.' As if I had merely forgotten to do such things. *Fear*: being born poor is the ultimate faux-pas.

5.  At times, not being entirely clear whether I stayed in my marriage for the sake of money (Helen has always contributed more financially) or whether money simply enabled the marriage to ride out its difficult patches. *Fear*: I have a mercenary soul.

6.  A bitter sense of having made some awful decisions, such as talking myself out of a very sensible property investment and then frittering money away on half-hearted ventures. We endured years of anxiety on account of this blunder. *Fear*: I am an economic fool.

7.  Having been very slow in earning a stable, bourgeois income. *Fear*: in financial matters I lack nous and character.

## iv. Finding the Right Company

Coming to know one's own intimate relationship with money, and disentangling the real money issues from those worries that are actually about something else, is a highly personal project. But it is not really a solitary one.

Talking openly about money is often taboo; it's too likely to lead to conflict, resentment, dishonesty. And even in friendship – at least in my experience – we don't generally talk much about the really intimate aspects of our financial lives.

But it's good to keep company with other people who are interested in improving the quality of their relationship with money. The project of 'stripping away' – of clarifying one's relationship with money, of growing in self-awareness and maturity – is intimate. It goes on in the heads and lives of individuals. Of course, it would be much easier if we were brought up in a society that was completely sane in this regard, and in which everyone took mature responsibility and long-term views about economic matters. But unfortunately this is not the case.

So we will benefit from involvement with communities of individuals who can help us become better versions of ourselves. In this case, to have a more sane and productive relationship with money.

But the key here turns out, surprisingly, not to be that by seeking out such communities we will find people who are obsessed with money or have a great interest in investment strategies (although this might be the case as well); rather, the crucial thing is sharing an interest in clarity and honesty – in disentangling our relationship with money. So how do we find the right company? What are we looking for in these individuals? Here are seven characteristics that might be desirable:

1. *People who encourage us to be realistic*: in Jane Austen's *Emma* the eponymous central character encourages her modest friend Harriet to fall in love with rich, high-status men; although, in their world, there is really no chance of her marrying such a man. This excessive aspiration threatens to spoil Harriet's chances of a happy life. We hold encouragement in such high regard that we forget that pumping up expectations is a means of making people miserable. In the end, Harriet is fortunate and makes a very sensible, appropriate marriage. Being realistic, in this case, wasn't about humiliating Harriet – it was about understanding her real needs. Emma didn't give adequate regard to what Harriet was really like; Harriet didn't at all need a rich marriage in order to flourish.

2. *People who don't use money as a way of humiliating others*: you occasionally encounter people who flaunt their wealth, with the implication that, if you haven't got as much as they have, then you don't fully exist in their eyes: you belong to a lesser species. Weirdly, it's not only those with a lot of money who use it to humiliate. It can be the wine waiter at a restaurant, when you order a cheaper bottle; or the receptionist at a hotel who makes you feel pathetic because you don't want to take a suite. It's not that they are well off. But what they imply is: I'll only

respect you if you spend a lot of money. You want to avoid these kinds of people.

3. *People who don't spread despair and resentment about money*: there are people whose fear of money gets disguised as contempt; and they want you to share their attitude. In their eyes, everything connected with making money is sordid and inequitable. There is always just enough evidence to support such convictions; they home in, relentlessly, on the bad news. Avoid these people. They will pollute your mind.

4. *People who encourage good habits*: they set a good example; they go without something that they want because it is unwise to spend the money; they buy second-hand clothes – and don't see this as shameful, but as sensible thrift.

5. *People who are open about their own economic experiences*: my own thinking about money has been much influenced by a friend in business, who was then very prosperous, talking me through his bankruptcy a decade before. It was deeply moving to hear of his love of his business, his desperate efforts to save it, the intense frustrations of not being able to do so and the bleak couple of years that followed, when he learned to survive on very little. The richness of the telling allowed this to enter my own imagination. The ideal is that we benefit from the experience of others – but this only happens when others

share their experience in a sufficiently full and honest way. It's quite rare to get behind the facade of another person's life. And our ideas about money are too often drawn from the surface appearance of the lives of others. But if one person sets the right example, others can follow. Openness breeds openness.

6. *People who listen – and don't project their situation onto yours*: there's a tendency amongst some people to say 'You should do this . . . ' when the real meaning is 'I do this . . . ' While the question of *why* we should both do the same is neither asked nor answered. Too often we use our own lives as the models for those of others. Listening means discovering what is actually going on for another person.

7. *People who open our minds to thinking more clearly about our situation, opportunities and difficulties; who demystify money and don't panic*: it's natural that one's own habits of mind and assumptions about life and the world feel as if they are natural, true and final. But the ideal money-friend encourages examination and revision of such *idées fixes*. But this isn't just a matter of brusquely dismissing fears or preoccupations, however irrational they may be. The truthfulness of the money-friend is balanced – and made useable – by their sympathy.

Like all friends, the money-friend helps us find a wiser, more realistic and more satisfying way of life.

# 3. What is Money?

We have been stripping away the symbolic meaning that people attach to money. What's left? What does it mean to see money for what it really is?

Money is essentially a means of exchange. It's the middle-man that our ancient systems of barter required in order to function. Money in itself is abstract. Pretty much anything can become money and money can become pretty much anything. For example, the devotion of one's time and talents to, say, organizing a distribution network for domestic appliances may become, amongst many other things, after-school tennis lessons for a child, or new bedroom curtains.

The fact is that the money in our bank account was once something else: work and enterprise. And that money will *become* something else: possessions and experiences.

Another standard definition of money says that money is a 'store of value'. This emphasizes that money can become many other things, *and at any time*.

A life with money can therefore be analysed in the following way:

1. How we turn money into possessions and experiences is incredibly important. Which possessions and experiences do you convert money into? How efficiently do you make the conversion?

2. How we turn work and enterprise into money is incredibly important. What effort or activity do *you* turn into money? How *much* money do you turn your efforts and activities into?

So:

In other words, what is the nature of the activities and efforts that are translated into money? And what is the nature of the possessions and experiences into which money is translated?

One common fear is that one's efforts are not, in themselves, sufficiently worthwhile. So even if you can translate those efforts into money, it's an unhappy deal because those efforts constitute a significant part of your existence. There is a lot of truth to the observation that we are what we do. Which is why it is so soul-destroying to spend a lot of time doing anything that you do not believe to be worthwhile.

Another common fear is that, even when there is, in principle, enough money, one is not actually able to translate it into good enough possessions and experiences. Money on its own does not show you how to do that.

So, ultimately the task in life is to translate efforts and activities that are inherently worthwhile into possessions and experiences that are themselves of lasting and true value. That is the ideal money cycle.

Our relationship with money becomes unhealthy when we remove it from this cycle. That happens when we stop seeing money as potential possessions and experiences – but rather see possessions and experiences as potential money. That's the situation of the person who does not see a painting, but only a price; who does not see an education, but only earning potential. And it happens when we see our activities just as ways of making money and not as activities to be evaluated for their inherent worth.

The underlying mistake in each case is the same. And it can be expressed with remarkable logical finality. Both treat *means* as if they were *ends*. Or, to put it another way, they treat a medium of exchange as if it were itself a real thing.

For instance, a house can be considered as an investment: it represents a certain quantity of money stored for a while in bricks and mortar (or glass and steel). And eventually it will be converted back into cash. The primary consideration all the time is money. The building is just a strange-looking *kind* of money. On the other hand, a house can be seen primarily as a home. It absorbs the experiences of those who dwell in it; it holds childhoods; it expresses personal style; it is the place where you enrich friendships. Of course, this takes money. But it is not all about money. Money is simply the means that makes possible these other good things.

We are talking about a psychological matter here. It is a question of attitude. In a person's mind, is a house primarily a home and secondarily an economic vehicle? Or is it primarily an economic concern and secondarily a place where life is lived? I think it is clear which attitude is better.

This perspective starts to probe the way our attitudes to money can help or hinder the pursuit of a good life.

# IV. Money and the Good Life

# 1. Money as an Ingredient

As we have seen, money, stripped back, is just a means of exchange. In other words money is an instrument. It sounds like a minor point, but this is extremely important, because it raises two huge questions: First: what is money a means *to*? Second: how can it be used efficiently and effectively to attain that end?

The simplest answer is that I want more money so that I can get specific things: a car, a flat, a holiday, a partner; status, love. That is, the things which will make me happy.

But there's a famous theory that suggests that money provides a diminishing return in terms of happiness:

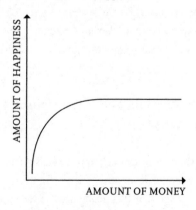

As you can see, the level of happiness rises quite quickly as people move from no money to modest amounts of money; then the line flattens off; beyond a certain level the line stops rising. (The average income would be around the middle of the money line.)

Actually, this should not surprise us. When we talk about happiness what do we have in mind? Probably a mixture of buoyancy and serenity: you feel elated but safe. And money has a real but diminishing relationship with these emotions.

Money can indeed buy things that make you feel serene: the plush hotel room, the country cottage. But there are many possible sources of serenity, such as a good temperament, stable relationships, taking physical exercise, possessing a religious belief, listening to music, that have no fixed relationship with money.

Money is linked to buoyancy. It can buy the accoutrements: the champagne, the red-carpet invitation, the airline ticket to exploration and glamour. Yet we know perfectly well that people can have these things and still feel sad and depressed.

If we need to spell out the explanation it goes like this: money can purchase the symbols but *not the causes* of serenity and buoyancy. In a straightforward way we must agree that money cannot buy happiness.

## i.  Why we should talk about flourishing rather than happiness

Serenity and buoyancy are obviously appealing. But they do not really capture what people seek from life.

Most people realize that they really need to do things for other people. There is a deep fear that one's life will be lived in vain – without making a contribution, or a benign difference, to the lives of others.

Doing valuable things doesn't always feel good at the time. You have to slog on, when you feel like giving up; risk annoying other people; accept the anxieties that come with competition; put your soul into things that might be rejected or are just plain difficult. Flourishing means getting on with the things that are important for you to do, exercising your capacities, actively trying to 'realize' what you care about and bring it into life. But these activities involve anxiety, fear of failure and setbacks, as well as a sense of satisfaction, occasional triumphs and moments of excitement.

A good life is still a life. It must involve its full share of suffering, loneliness, disappointment and coming to terms with one's own mortality and the deaths of those one loves. To live a life that is good *as a life* involves all this.

Flourishing captures what we actually aspire to: the best use of our capacities and abilities; involvement in things we take to be worthwhile; the formation and expression of one's best self.

That's why flourishing is a more accurate term than happiness for what we want from life.

## ii. What's the relationship between money and flourishing?

Well, it's true enough that more money doesn't make us much happier, in the sense of inner buoyancy and serenity, at least not for very long and not to a very high degree. So if that's really what you are after, seeking more and more money clearly isn't a very good strategy.

But if we think of flourishing, then money plays quite a different role.

What money is really good at is enabling action and allowing us to obtain material possessions. Money is a source of power and influence.

These are not the direct routes to buoyancy and serenity. But they are intimately linked to flourishing. Because they directly help you to make a difference, pursue the things you care about, develop your talents and foster the talents of others.

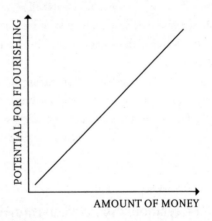

Potentially, flourishing continues to rise as money increases – the line does not flatten off as it does in the money/happiness graph we looked at before.

Flourishing is open-ended. And an increase in money always increases possible flourishing.

But money is not the sole cause of flourishing. *Money is an ingredient – a resource.*

## iii. Money as an ingredient

There are very few things you can make with money alone. But there are lots of things you can't easily make *without* money. The logic of ingredients is familiar and simple – but we keep on forgetting it when we think about money.

Money brings about good consequences – helps us live valuable lives – *only* when joined with 'virtues'. Virtues are good abilities of mind and character.

| Project | Money Brings | Virtues Required | Money Without Virtues Gets |
|---------|--------------|------------------|----------------------------|
| *A fine home* | Choice of property and location, choice of furnishings, appliances, access to help. | Style, a good eye, close relationships, a convivial spirit, decisiveness, persistence, good taste. | Vulgar house interiors and pretentious or bleak socializing environment. |
| *A good holiday* | Freedom of manoeuvre, options about where to stay and eat and what to do. | Sense of purpose, self-knowledge, canniness, resilience, spirit of adventure, cultural sensitivity. | Superficial entertainment, lacklustre memories, shallow, inauthentic cultural experiences, self-denial and dissatisfaction. |
| *A good education* | Extra chances, opportunity for longer periods of study, more choice, access to help. | Will and desire to learn, proper vision of self-improvement, sense of intellectual enterprise and enthusiasm, pursuit of wisdom and confidence. | An uninspired mind, lack of motivation and fulfilment, life of inconsiderate privilege; guilt or denial (boringness). |

Flourishing is not selfish, or greedy, or anti-social in the way that the remorseless pursuit of one's own feelings of serenity or elation can often be. The genuine flourishing of individuals is of collective benefit. That's because the good exercise of abilities must promote general well-being, while my private buoyancy and serenity may add nothing at all to the lives of others.

## iv. How much do I need?

This is a very important question – and we should not shrug it off with 'as much as you can get'.

We can only ask 'How much do I need?' when we think of money clearly as an ingredient. Pursuing that enquiry means we have to ask:

1. What are my real objectives? (They might be a happy home, the good development of one's mind, rich engagement with the world.)
2. What (apart from money) is important for attaining these things?
3. What does money contribute?

It's only then that the money aspect can be clarified. Because then we can see what money is actually needed for. Writing down your own answers to these questions is important.

I'll be exploring this in more detail later, but first I want to explore how the 'ingredient' approach might help us with the intimate problem of how money interacts with love and sex.

# 2. Jane Austen's Theory of Marriage

## i. Is money connected to love and sex?

Using the ingredient approach we can see that money can play an important part in forming good relationships with other people – and in making love succeed.

We tend to feel a bit awkward about mixing up material needs with our spiritual hopes and romantic longings. We feel pressured into saying there's no connection. How crude – one fears – to think there might be. We are heirs to a romantic tradition that tells us not to worry too much about such things. This way of thinking focuses our attention on the star cases: a poor guy who is very appealing versus the rich man who is pompous and shallow; a happy impoverished couple contrasted with a miserable rich couple. Yet one of our most famous 'romance' novelists had an altogether more pragmatic view of how money should relate to love.

## ii. Jane Austen's answer

In the long run, and for most people, love (and by implication sex, although Austen is too refined to talk about this directly) benefits from a healthy economic condition. This isn't a law of nature, of course, and there are exceptions.

The big temptation is to read this the other way round. Jane Austen is not saying that on its own money gets you love and a good sex life. She supports the ingredient approach to money: it may be very important when combined with other good things; on its own it gets you nowhere at all. The wealthiest individual in all her works is Mr Rushworth, the feeble-minded landowner in *Mansfield Park*. His marriage is a complete failure.

Jane Austen believes that strong, stable, satisfying relationships require several good foundations, only one of which is economic. She's also quite specific about the amount of money people need. For instance, in *Sense and Sensibility* she marries Elinor Dashwood to Edward Ferrars. They have a joint income of about £850 a year, which is the lowest income of all her married heroines. But it is still quite a lot by the ordinary standards of the time. And a significant part of the story turns on their having enough – and what the proper definition of 'enough' really is. We have been shown, furthermore, that these two people have the qualities of mind and character that will allow them to 'meet all their wants' on that income.

The anti-hero of that novel, Willoughby, has enough money for a very comfortable style of life. But he is extravagant and improvident. When he really falls in love – with Marianne Dashwood – marriage is impossible because he has wasted his resources. Willoughby now has to marry money to clear his debts, and Marianne is not a good enough catch from a financial point of view. Jane Austen provides him with a shrewish heiress, as the perfect punishment.

Charlotte Lucas, the Bennets' neighbour in *Pride and Prejudice*, marries the comfortably-off Mr Collins. But a good relationship is impossible because Collins lacks so many other necessary qualities.

Jane Austen is trying to teach us a lesson: money is *necessary*, but not *sufficient*. But she is also advising us that the question of *how much* is needed is crucial. When you say money is important, it tends to generate the impression that you mean 'the more the better'. But that's not her point at all.

The ingredient approach forces us to pay attention to proportion. If you have the right attitude, a little money goes a long way; if you have the wrong attitude, even a lot of money won't help you.

Marrying just for money is not at all the same as taking seriously the economic basis of a relationship. But – doesn't this go against the basic idea that we should follow our hearts when it comes to relationships? It sounds mercenary.

Well, yes it does a bit. But that's the conclusion you should reach when you look at relationships. Long-lasting, stable enough, bearable enough, relationships are complex human achievements. They have something in common with friendship and something in common with a business partnership.

So, your prospective marriage partner says, 'If it wasn't for my money, you wouldn't want to marry me.' What it is important for both parties to understand is that a marriage is quite a complicated undertaking. The reasonable response is: 'I would *want* to marry you irrespective of the finances. But I would regard it as unwise to marry you. Not everything I want to do is – in the long run – a good idea.' Consider it from the other side. Not every good idea is emotionally appealing. It might be a very good idea for me to marry someone who has sensible financial instincts and solid assets, even if the relationship is a little less appealing in other ways.

The goal of a relationship is that both people flourish together. And because money is a crucial ingredient in flourishing, it is a crucial ingredient in marriage.

## iii. What about sex?

The unhelpful image is of the wealthy gross man who gets the favours of a gorgeous partner only because of his money. But money has other, more benign, connections with sexual happiness:

1. Money is for some people an aphrodisiac. This is not mysterious. Money stands imaginatively for status and future success. We should expect these things to be linked to sexual appetite.

2. Money buys luxury, privacy and sensual stimulation. In modern relationships sexual behaviour is compromised by lack of time and opportunity. If only we could go to an elegant hotel, leave the children with a babysitter, get the clothes and haircuts that make us feel good about ourselves . . .

3. Money reduces the fragility of a relationship. When there's a joint investment in good assets, it's harder – though obviously not impossible – to separate. Good

relationships contain many distressing episodes when someone feels like walking out the door. But money gives a reason to stay that encourages the couple to overcome their temporary troubles.

4. More speculatively, it might be that having more money tends to make people a little more relaxed about human nature. So the occasional infidelity or furtive pleasure won't be particularly shocking or so much of a problem. (But I honestly don't know whether this is the case.)

These considerations help explain the importance of money in marriage. Sexual unhappiness is such a large factor in what goes wrong in relationships; so anything that helps with sex helps with marriage. The partnership of marriage allows for an unequal burden of wealth creation: ideally, one person who is very good at creating wealth gets into partnership with someone who is very good at flourishing – they have the skills and virtues that enable them to make the best of opportunities for themselves and for those around them.

This is a fine arrangement because it allows for a degree of specialization, while it spreads the advantages. So each person enjoys the advantages of both wealth-creation and flourishing. And it suggests that in looking for the 'right' partner we should not be afraid to take into consideration money, and attitudes to money.

My own experience is that money worries can cause terrible conflicts in relationships. I fear I have damaged Helen's life by not making more money. And there are stylistic clashes: I like being lavish; she's much more restrained. For instance, I like the idea of going to fancy restaurants; she prefers the modest family-run place round the corner, or chicken soup at home. (And this is all the harder to deal with because our earnings point in the opposite directions to these personal tastes. Financially speaking, she 'deserves' the starched napkins, whereas I don't. I confess a part of me still resents this.) Sometimes we all want to shout: 'Why can't you be more like me?' But I've had to recognize that it would have been fatal to have got together with someone who was like me. Together, 'Girl-version-of-me' and I would have sunk in a sea of credit-card debt. The price of salvation has been conflict. But the suffering is much less serious than the alternative.

# 3. Envy as Education

Well Walk, in Hampstead, is one of the most attractive old streets in the northern suburbs of London. I particularly like the end nearest Hampstead Heath. You sense the presence of woodland and meadows but you feel part of a grand city. It's quite a narrow street; the houses are companionably close and pleasantly varied. I'd love to live there. I dream of a big ground-floor flat with high ceilings, a library with elegant bookcases; the children's bedrooms down a corridor, round a corner; an Aga in the kitchen; a garden with a high hedge and a swathe of rich cool grass; arguing with clever friends over a bottle of white wine on summer evenings; withdrawing into a big sofa in front of the fire in the winter.

I envy the people who live here.

This is a representative moment in the private history of money experiences. You see something you really want – which speaks to your soul of your own well-being and the flourishing of the people you most care about. It is very disturbing because you realize that you absolutely can't get this thing.

In one way it's a very good and reasonable dream. Leave property prices aside for a moment. What I've pictured is, I think, quite a decent sketch of family happiness. It's not greedy or ostentatious. I'm sure my wife and children would love to move there. That kind of environment would really suit us.

But all this is wildly beyond my current financial reach. I'd need (at a guess) five times my current income. It's (only just) a conceivable project. But I'd have to entirely remake myself as a getter of money before I could spend that way. It would take a different kind of career, a different attitude to work. Retraining, reshaping, risk, and a long time.

# What to do with this kind of experience

## 1. Take it seriously

It happens a lot – flicking through a magazine, I glance at an article about a woman who has: (a) a successful practice at the bar; (b) two children; (c) sane and significant ideas about politics; (d) a holiday home in Burgundy; (e) fantastic taste in work suits.

Watching people at an airport, I envy (a) someone's apparent absorption in an interesting book; (b) their easy self-containment and serenity; (c) their nice luggage; (d) their simple, elegant clothes; (e) that a sexy-looking person comes by – and it's their partner; and (*f*) that they are strolling together into business class.

Instead of dismissing this kind of experience as just fantasy, or endlessly repeating it, one should examine it, learn from it. Not rejecting it means, to start with, accepting a bit of pain. I've imagined something genuinely good and I can't have it. I'm not going to tell myself that it isn't good, simply because I can't have it. This sentiment of rejection emerges – a bit crudely – when genuinely good things are dismissed as 'posh' or 'snobby'.

Mourning is a helpful concept here. When a person dies, we know we have to take the sorrow seriously. We don't pretend that the person didn't die or that it doesn't matter. In a less intense but still important matter, we should mourn the loss of other things we love. Well Walk really deserves love, and one should be saddened by the rarity of such places and by the loss of the life that (imagination tells us) could have been.

## 2. Respect the distance between this kind of experience and its psychological neighbour – the fantasy of riches

If I suddenly got a billion pounds, I'd . . . buy a large tract of land in Perthshire and build my perfect home: a more domestic version of Blenheim Palace, smaller and with a lovely garden in the main courtyard. I'd not send my children to school but have them educated at home. I'd pretend to be vexed when they tore through the salons or rode their bikes down the long library but I'd actually revel in their freedom around the Claudes and Poussins, and smile when they scratched the furniture. Buy more! I'd have a porphyry swimming pool, a jet, a palazzo in Venice, a love-nest in New York . . .

What's the difference between this and the dream of an apartment on Well Walk? The palace is pure fantasy. I actually have no idea at all what would happen if I suddenly had vast wealth; perhaps I'd become a monster of greed and self-indulgence. It's an escapist amusement. Its function is to allow me to ignore reality, for a little while.

But the experience in Well Walk is not escapist, although, in a dismissive frame of mind, I might be tempted to think it is. It has something useful (even if a bit difficult) to tell me about the actual ingredients of a good life. If we lump together the experience of Well Walk and the daydream of the easy billion, we miss what Well Walk has to say.

## 3. Be creative

In the case of Well Walk, the script is already clear. It's obvious how you are supposed to use the elements that the script provides to make a good life. It's the clarity and reliability of the script that appeals. That's why the allure is strong – because you can see clearly how you would be happy there; or why it would be nice to be like the couple at the airport or the mother–barrister.

Trying to copy them exactly can't be the solution. And it isn't how inspiration is best taken from the things we admire. Imagine the case of a novelist who loves Tolstoy's *War and Peace*. That great work happens to be about the impact on a group of aristocratic families of Napoleon's invasion of Russia in 1812. So the modern novelist might think: 'That's what I should write about, too.' He starts reading up about Moscow in the early nineteenth century. But that's almost certainly not the right approach. Below the surface, *War and Peace* is inspiring because of the way Tolstoy enters the inner lives of his characters and the warmth of his sympathy. And these wonderful qualities can be separated from the specific historical setting of the action. Instead of mimicking the surface features, we should try to reproduce the underlying virtues.

The things that grab our initial attention are like Tolstoy's historical setting. The luggage, the business-class ticket, the street in Hampstead, the holiday home in Burgundy and the successful legal career – these are only surfaces; they are not really what we should be trying to reproduce.

What matters is what lies behind them: the sense of serenity; the cosiness; the ideas of accomplishment and competence, good organization and a warm family life. Our modern novelist might end up writing about a group of school teachers in Glasgow in the 1970s. And the book could be 'Tolstoyan' – because of its approach to character and experience – without so much as a hint of Russia or Napoleon.

Things seem to have more value when they are endorsed by others and thus gain cachet. So, rather than letting lack of money hold you back, you need to think creatively around what you already have. Don't avoid envy. Don't we all have fantasies along the lines of 'Oh if only I lived there or had those things my life would be amazing'? But when you analyse what's really speaking to you, it often turns out that it's not really a desire for more wealth but the idea of escaping some of the more mundane parts of your current life; that feeling of 'starting afresh' and being a slightly different, slightly better person.

# V. Creating Order

# 1. Need versus Want

The knowledge of what we really need is precious. Clarity, here, feeds resolution: one's energies find a better focus.

Typically we invoke the need–desire distinction to lower our hopes and school ourselves to more modest (and more sane and more achievable) goals. Do you really need a beach house or a sports-car or dinner at a famous restaurant? No – these are merely desires. They are nice, but not necessary. Hence, if we want to be wise about money we should resist the impulse to follow our desires and concentrate instead on getting what we need.

Need is deeper – bound up with the serious narrative of one's life. 'Do I need this?' is a way of asking: how important is this thing, how central is it to my becoming a good version of myself; what is it actually *for* in my life? This interrogation is designed to distinguish needs from mere wants. And that's a good distinction to make.

But it is important to see that this is not the same as the 'modest versus grand' distinction. Our needs are not always for the smaller, lesser, cheaper thing.

A fine violinist might need a bow that has a stratospheric price tag. But it's right to call this a need – and not just a desire. I should emphasize here that 'need' doesn't mean you need this thing to *survive*. The violinist needs the bow because the bow has a central role to play in this person's life. The musician has devoted a large part of his or her life to acquiring the skills and sensitivity that such an expensive, refined bow is responsive to and rewards. Therefore, this object will come to hold an important and deep place in that person's life. They would misunderstand themselves if they said, 'Oh, it's rather expensive, I don't really need it.'

Therefore, it does not follow that you can always afford what you need. But then this gives a proper and deep motive for making more money. Ideally, the right income is that which allows us to meet our true needs.

When we understand need in this way, it reveals what goes wrong when people pursue luxuries that they don't *really* need. These purchases will not help them either develop or flourish. That doesn't necessarily mean that they are worthless, but that the individual in question lacks the skill or sensitivity to use them properly.

Greed is one of the central terms of the modern ethical vocabulary. Greed is not the desire for more than other people have – which is how we tend to use it. It's not necessarily greedy to want a beautiful house, if you love it for its beauty – even though this might mean wanting something much more expensive than most people can afford.

## i.  How do you differentiate between need and desire?

The way to make this distinction is to ask what *need* and *desire* each are a part of. Ultimately one is asking: how *wise* – intelligent, practically important – is it that I pursue this thing? And the strength of one's immediate longing is only a very rough and sometimes very misleading guide to answering that question. Where does the object under consideration go in my life? How big a role should it play in my life? How central/essential is it to the project of living a good life and being a good version of myself?

Ask yourself 'How good will it be for me to have this thing in my life?' In other words, the need/want distinction goes right to the heart of questions about identity, ethics and the meaning of life. You can't address money properly unless you think about these things seriously.

For instance, I've been looking at an eighteenth-century side table in the window of a local antique shop. In our sitting room there's a sofa opposite the fireplace. On either side of the sofa we have a side table with a table lamp on it. It's an arrangement that I really like. When we have people to dinner we start with drinks in there. I like that it is an elegant, rather formal room. I feel that it expresses an important part of my character and that it conveys something quite deep about how I see life. It expresses an idea about social life and about conversation. But the thing is, the two tables we have don't go all that well together. One is rather better than the other. The one for sale in the shop window would be a much better fit with the overall pattern and style of the room. So, on balance I'd say that we need that table. Although there is a completely obvious sense in which we can live without it, I think that it is right that we should have it. There's something substantial I want to do with it in my life. This is not random acquisitiveness. It's a part of creating an environment that embodies values that I live by and take seriously. I appreciate the particular qualities and merits of the table.

However, I've decided that I can't afford the table. But I don't want to give up wanting it. I don't want to school myself into the belief that, because I can't afford it, it doesn't matter whether I have it or not.

I need this table, even though I could live without it.

It is important to understand that 'need/want' does not map onto 'basic/refined' or 'cheap/luxurious'. And for powerful reasons. 'Need/want' is a psychological distinction relative to individual flourishing and the pursuit of one's best self. 'Basic/refined' is a distinction about the level of complexity of an object. 'Cheap/expensive' is a distinction to do with price and demand.

The core strategy I am recommending, then, is counter-intuitive (but important): we have to work out our needs first, without reference to price. It's entirely possible that you may not be able to afford certain things you need. It is also possible that, even when something is affordable and wanted, it might still be a bad idea to purchase it. In fact, that is what opens up resources for the more important projects. So, one should develop an inner hierarchy here. Which is, in effect, an essay, a report on one's own flourishing and development imagined across a life.

## ii. Higher, middle and lower needs

It's a striking misfortune of modern culture that *needs* tend to be associated with physical survival. Basically, you have a deep right to what you need, while getting what you want is another matter entirely.

Needs can be divided into three basic types:

| Higher<br>Noble/Intrinsic | Middle<br>Social/Comparative | Lower<br>Basic |
| --- | --- | --- |
| The things you need in order to flourish as an individual, to be the best authentic version of yourself. | What one requires to gain the respect of one's society – which is relative to that society. | What one requires in order to survive as a citizen – healthy food, safe shelter, employment. |

Higher needs include: deep friendships; a mission in life; personal style; emotional maturity.

Middle needs include: a well-paid job; fashionable clothes; exotic travel; acquaintance with high-status people.

A higher need may be quite difficult to describe and identify, because it is more complex and more elusive. But it is still a need – that is, it is still vital to your flourishing. But we often subordinate these needs to more obvious demands.

## iii. Distinguishing between middle and higher needs

Middle-order needs of sociability, status in the community and connectedness to other people – being plugged into your society – are often very closely connected to money. In a way these are the most frequently coveted goods. It is precisely in these terms that money and happiness appear to be linked, because money is a direct means to getting more middle-order goods. But – ironically – middle-order goods are subject to a vanishing horizon. That is, as you get more of them you become conscious of how little you have.

In *Remembrance of Things Past*, Marcel Proust gives the perfect example: You meet a boring, annoying person, and are filled with a longing to go to the right parties, where you might meet the right people. Eventually you go to the party, but the right people there won't invite you to their parties. Eventually you get invited, but realize that the host also gives much more coveted lunches. Eventually you get invited – and meet the boring, annoying person you were stuck with at the first party.

The crucial developmental step in the economic lives of individuals and societies is their ability to cross from the pursuit of middle-order goods to higher-order goods. Sometimes we need to lessen our attachment to the middle needs like status and glamour in order to concentrate on higher things. This doesn't take more money; it takes more independence of mind.

Higher needs are often met in indirect ways. What we really need is time, mental space, understanding, a level of engagement with the minds and lives of others.

## iv. The indirect costs of higher needs

Reading *Mansfield Park* (to continue the Jane Austen theme) or *War and Peace* requires not just a copy of the work, which can be had for almost nothing, but the time to devote to reading it slowly and thoughtfully; the inner space to be able to go to bed an hour early, or to lie in the bath or sit in a cafe or park – and not be fretting and prowling anxiously around. And one needs the resources to dwell on the content. Because these works can't meet your higher needs unless you bring a lot of yourself into engagement with them.

Higher needs are not high-flown or pretentious. The need to be understood, to create things of value, to meet the inner lives of others, to refine one's emotions: these are everyday concerns. And they are played out – met or left unmet – as we go through our days trying to address our more obvious needs.

## v. Higher needs and status

An elegant house in a gracious street meets a higher need, although it is often confused with a middle-order social need. The words 'posh' and 'snobbish' often illuminate this confusion. They refer to social pretensions – that is, a problem of middle-order needs. A person wants to feel socially superior, so they buy a big house; they want to feel that they are mixing with the top people, so they go to a fancy restaurant or get tickets to the opera; they want to be regarded as cultured, so they collect art. And essentially the criticism of 'posh' and 'snobbish' is that they are doing these things only as a means of gaining status. And in so far as that is what they are doing, the criticism is right. But it is generally a crude instrument of attack. It does not recognize that the engagement with the opera, the restaurant, the house or the works of art can be driven by higher needs. The line of criticism basically is that 'higher needs' are always *really* about status. And that is false; but it is a tricky point because quite often people do buy into the assets that should serve higher needs only for the sake of status. But the solution is not to come down hard on the objects themselves, but to get much more perceptive about the kinds of motives at stake, and much more adept at distinguishing a worthy from an unworthy motive. And the key to that distinction lies in having a clear conception of the difference between middle-order and higher-order concerns.

It may well be that status-seeking is an inescapable impulse of human nature. If this is true then we should seek to reform it, rather than vainly try to eliminate it. Reform would link status to the right things. It's not wrong to admire someone, or to think of them as enviable. What we must ask is why we admire, and what it is that we envy. If someone has high status because they are wise, generous, sensitive to beauty and bring out the best in others – then absolutely their high status is deserved. If we envy those qualities in them, and therefore seek to acquire them ourselves, then envy is playing a productive role in life. But if we confer status on the basis of what kind of credit card an individual has, or where he or she went to school or what kind of car they drive, then status does not align with merit. In general we tend to regard envy as corrosive and to be avoided. But it can be valuable – if our envy points us in the right direction.

Status is a group phenomenon; it occurs because, within groups, people do tend to look up or look down, to admire or disdain. Some individuals are collectively regarded as being the best kind of person and others are collectively seen as lacking. But how status is distributed is variable. In a crude and mean-spirited group, status will be accorded in horrible ways. The most thuggish, callous and stupidly self-assertive person will have the most status. In a refined and serious group, status will reflect the inner merits of an individual.

What this means is that we desperately need to find the right kind of company. We cannot, as individuals, control the status-giving processes of whole societies. In our elective circles, however, we can hope to find and create a good distribution of status.

Status anxiety feeds money worries. Status in itself is neither good nor bad. It all depends on what is taken to indicate status – that can range from utterly superficial (make of car, colour of hair) to the wise and profound (insight, kindness). Our duty to ourselves and to other people is to try to nudge the basis on which status is attributed, shifting it from the superficial to the profound end of the spectrum. And as we do this, we find that we worry less about money and give our thoughts to the thing that should occupy our attention: the real basis of good lives.

# 2. How Much Money Do I Need?

Try to describe what you actually need in order to live a flourishing life – including taking responsibility for others. It's important to be explicit when undertaking this exercise. It's not yet about cost.

The desire to be realistic means that we cut off avenues before we have had time to think them through and work out what version of them might be viable. In other words we tend to be realistic about what we can afford. But first we should be realistic about what we need.

Actually, there's a refining process, by which you identify what are the fantasy elements and what are real – this takes time, but can lead to crucial gains in self-knowledge or collective knowledge. So, for most people, it's not going to make any sense to say 'I need a private jet'. Because, although that would be great fun, not many people truly need to travel at maximum speed very often in order to flourish.

Now try to *cost* these things that you need for a flourishing life.

Over the page is a breakdown of levels of expenditure for the flourishing of my family. It is an attempt to work out how much money my wife and I actually need, year by year.

| Need | Items | Minimal (AU$) | True Need (AU$) | Expensive Ideal (AU$)* |
|------|-------|---------------|-----------------|------------------------|
| A convenient place to live | A nice house (old style we like, big enough); suitable location for work and children's education | 27,000 (as annual cost of ownership) | 55,000 | 125,000 |
| | Annual maintenance and improvements | 1,000 | 5,000 | 10,000 |
| | Garden maintenance and improvements | Do it ourselves | 2,500 | 10,000 |
| | Interior contents (paintings, antiques, white goods etc.) | Ok with what we have | 12,500 | 50,000 |
| | Utilities (insurance, IT, phones, electricity, water) | 6,500 | 6,500 | 10,000 |
| | Rates | 650 | 1,250 | 1,850 |
| Travel (other than work) | Family trip to Europe (economy air fare, nice place to rent) | Don't go | 24,000 | 85,000 |
| Sport and fitness | Tennis club membership and fees, yoga, Pilates, sailing lessons | 2,000 | 5,000 | 5,000 |
| Children's education | | 5,000 | 24,000 | 24,000 |

| Need | Items | Minimal (AU$) | True Need (AU$) | Expansive Ideal (AU$)* |
|------|-------|---------------|-----------------|------------------------|
| Saving for children's future education | | 2,000 | 20,000 | 85,000 |
| Children's toys | | 500 | 2,000 | 2,000 |
| Clothes | | 1,000 | 3,500 | 12,500 |
| Food and drink | | 7,000 | 10,000 | 25,000 |
| Eating out | And babysitter | Stay in | 2,500 | 5,000 |
| Pension contributions | | Deal with this later | 22,000 | 100,000 |
| TOTAL | Income needed after tax | 52,650 | 195,750 | 550,350 |

* At the time of going to press £1.00 equated to 1.50AU$.

Rather than try to cut back on expenses, the ambition here is to be as accurate as possible about the things one needs for one's flourishing – fully accepting that one may not be able to afford certain things that one actually needs. It's painful. When I look at this account I get a bit desperate. We're much closer to the 'minimal' column than the 'true needs' one, and the 'expansive ideal' feels very far away. But the point of the exercise isn't meant to be self-humiliation. It's meant to be a sober reality check. With this in view we can go on to consider what we need to do in order to get closer to meeting our true needs.

I want to look at a couple of cases in which people I know have adjusted their way of life to reflect their needs. It's not that, on balance, they now spend less. It's rather that they have focused their expenditure on what's most important to them.

## i. Derek and Jasmine

Derek and Jasmine have long been fascinated by architecture. But it's not just that they like looking at buildings or reading interiors magazines. They want to live in interesting buildings. But in London this was completely beyond their means, so, about three years ago, they took a big decision to move to rural France. They were trying to find a place where they could live in what would really be quite a grand house, given their fairly limited resources.

Moving was difficult in some ways, because it meant leaving some close friends, and Derek had to change career. They were gambling on self-knowledge. They took the view that it was really important for them to live in a very old, fairly big house with an orchard. Near London that would have cost millions of pounds. In Normandy, the price tag was radically lower. But they had to believe that this kind of environment was so important to them that they should seek it out – even though that meant giving up on other things.

## ii. The Jennings Family

The Jenningses decided to give up celebrating Christmas and birthdays so that they could go on extremely interesting holidays. It was really quite hard for their children who had to cope with many awkward moments amongst their peer groups – they never had new bikes, they didn't have the status-giving gadgets and complicated toys their friends did. The gamble, in their case, was on the belief that spending time together walking across Scotland or visiting the classical ruins of Turkey would do more for their collective flourishing than getting a lot of presents.

In each of these cases there was a commitment to something that cost a lot of money. Derek and Jasmine and the Jenningses were asking themselves, in a strenuous way: *what is it really important for us to do or to have?* We should take guidance from their example:

*Ask yourself first*: In the long run, what are the activities, experiences and possessions that I should be concentrating on? Is a holiday more important than presents? Is the kind of house I live in more important than where it is? Amongst the great number of things we want, what are the most important for our flourishing? (These should be classed as needs.)

*Then ask*: What wants do I have that are, in fact, less central to my long-term well-being? It can be painful making these decisions. They require downgrading certain wants and leaving them unfulfilled. But that is the price of concentrating money resources in the most important places.

# 3. Price versus Value

One problem with the costing process is that a lot of things do not have set prices. Suppose it is really important to you to live in nicely furnished rooms. What does that cost? Well, in part it depends on your skill at finding and purchasing things you like. The same chest of drawers might cost four times as much in one outlet as in another.

*Price* is a public matter – a negotiation between supply and demand. A thing's price is set in competition. So the price of a car is determined by how much some people want it, how much they are willing to pay, and how ready the manufacturer is to sell. It's a public activity: lots of people are involved in the process, but your voice is almost never important in setting the price.

*Value*, on the other hand, is a personal, ethical and aesthetic judgement – assigned finally by individuals, and founded on their perceptiveness, wisdom and character.

How much value is yielded by a given quantity of money? What is the 'value return'? We know this varies hugely. Some people are able to turn comparatively small quantities of money into wonderful experiences. They have marvellous holidays, they entertain charmingly, they have interesting paintings and you'd like to steal their furniture. And they do this on a smaller budget than you'd imagine (or than you or other people could). These characters are resourceful. They're not necessarily trying to save money.

Don't bother about a carpet; do buy a nice shirt; no clutter; take great care painting the walls. Wilhelm Ferdinand Bendz, *The Artist's Brothers*, c.1830.

Here are the secrets of these resourceful characters:

1.  They know what is important in creating an experience and what isn't. For instance, at a dinner party most people don't really care what the wine is so long as it is drinkable.

2.  They don't follow fashion – which inflates prices. They judge objects, ideas and people on their intrinsic merits (rather than on the reflection of their status – what others think).

3.  They have good taste: they can home in on what they really like and why they like it, and therefore identify it in less obvious places and cases.

4.  They are creative: they look at potential and are not worried about taking responsibility for realizing potential. They have the inner drive and flair to do this.

These qualities – which are not directly taught in economics classes – are crucially important to our economic lives.

Money is (to say it again) a means of exchange. Money needs to be exchanged for – or translated into – value. But that exchange is often an art, and only sometimes a science. This art entails wisdom and intelligence in getting the things that matter to you. For instance, what is the cost of a dinner party? Of a beautiful room? Of a great painting? Of attractive clothes? These don't have fixed costs, because they depend on our creativity, resourcefulness and independence of mind.

Suppose, however, you're saying to yourself, 'That's all very well, but I'm just not that creative'? I don't think the lesson here depends on having the eye of an interior decorator or an art critic. It depends on following a fairly down-to-earth process. Take a selection of images that you like – images that speak to you. Then ask: what are they really saying to me? For instance: I'd always wanted to have a matching set of old teacups and saucers. But I couldn't afford them. Then I saw a picture of quite a messy house, with a big table on which there were lots of mismatched old cups. The mess didn't appeal, but it made me realize that matching wasn't so important – and individually the cups and saucers are a lot cheaper. And now, about ten years later, I have quite a collection of individual pieces and get a reliable, everyday thrill from using them. It's a tiny instance, of course. But it illustrates the process. The hints are out there. If only we pay attention to them.

Let me give an example on a bigger scale. A house round the corner from us was recently for sale. It's quite different from our place. We live in an old building that's been adapted at various times; it doesn't fit the modern sales-pitch template. It isn't 'flooded with light'; it doesn't have a 'huge family kitchen'; it's not 'an entertainer's dream' (although we have had some lovely dinner parties). We occasionally get pitying looks from our neighbours.

The house round the corner isn't beautiful; it's about the same size as ours and has a smaller garden. But (to continue the language of real estate) it ticks the boxes. It sold for half as much again as our house is worth. The difference equals my entire income for several years. In a way it's just a stroke of luck. We really like certain things (odd nooks and corners, unexpected changes in level, touches of architectural grandeur) that don't command a high market price where we happen to live. But discovering that our house would sell for less than the one round the corner doesn't make it any less valuable *to us*.

# 4. Longing and Fear

My father used to keep all his financial records in a desk with a folding top. From time to time I'd catch him opening the front flap slightly and stuffing in a fistful of torn envelopes and crumpled papers. In the drawers below were drifts of bills, documents, official forms, scrawled letters and lists, stamped dockets, pages torn from notebooks. I saw my father's shame and guilt as he dumped another heap in the swamp.

I assumed it was easy to keep one's records in perfect order. Aged almost 14 – with an annual income of £26, with no taxes or bills to pay and nothing involving money to be ashamed or frightened of – I kept a lucid record of my occasional expenditures.

Here are the first few lines from October 1980:

| from September | | I've got | £20.75 |
|---|---|---|---|
| 3rd | got 50p from grandpa | now I've got | £21.25 |
| 6th | bought *Think Like a Grandmaster*, £2.99 | I've got left | £18.26 |
| 10th | got 50p from grandpa | now I've got | £18.76 |

My eye would linger contentedly on the lines. The handwriting was beautiful. Yet I now know only too well the nightmare labyrinth of my own money drawer: to be opened only in gloom and anguish. I shall never be able to find the information or documents I need.

The more urgent the demand, the more frantic the search, the more confused the piles become. The spiral accelerates downwards. My life is ruined. I am filled with rage and despair. I want to throw armfuls of paper out of the window and just submit to pending disaster – divorce, penury or prison.

But *why*? Why is it so very hard for me to maintain a simple, clear and manageable system of records? Why can't I give myself a clean view of where I stand, where I'm going, how much I've spent, how much I've saved (or owe)? Do I find sorting things out, keeping records, filing documents and filling in forms *boring*? Am I just *lazy*? In principle, I quite like bounded, fiddly, repetitive tasks. I have to stop myself playing Sudoku and I over-organize jigsaw pieces (I like sorting them by the number and pattern of lobes and indents). When I play Monopoly I'm fanatical about keeping my money and cards in perfect order. So, although my first reaction (and that of those I'm close to) is to blame myself for being lazy, and to insist that I get on with it even though it is boring, laziness and a tendency to be easily bored are not really the causes of my difficulties. That's because laziness and finding things boring are symptoms, not causes.

The cause is this: it feels psychologically dangerous to go near this particular issue, just as one instinctively draws one's hand back from an electric hotplate. Psychologically – spiritually, imaginatively – we draw back from those things that we feel will kill our souls. In other words, the fear is deep and important. It has to be overcome; but one can't overcome it if one misunderstands it.

I am afraid of organizing my money drawer – in the way that I'm afraid of heights. I know that I should not be; but the fear feels exactly the way real fear does. The person who suffers from vertigo feels as

I felt very little pity.

if they are about to plunge to their death – even though they are safe. But it is a genuinely terrifying experience.

The fantasy solution is – maddeningly, but very logically – money. I'd feel better about my relationship with money if I had more money. But I can't get more money because I feel bad about my relationship with money. Chaos is the result of an unhappy relationship with money. And the confusion and anxiety that chaos brings then makes things even worse. It's a central (but currently neglected) task of art to help us address and overcome our spiritual problems as they are played out in daily life.

At first sight the Roman poet Virgil might seem like an unlikely person to turn to for help. In the early years of the Empire (Augustus was his greatest patron), Virgil wrote a series of poems about farming, the *Georgics*. They constitute an instruction manual, telling you when to plough, how to keep bees and train vines. Their importance, here and now, lies in the way Virgil shows the dignity, charm and goodness of the small but worrisome quandaries and the humble, routine activities of resource management. It's a book for people who are not instinctive farmers, but for those who think they might well be lazy or bored – and who shy away from having to think about all these different things at once.

Here's how he does it: some tasks, he is saying, can be appreciated for themselves. You separate them from their consequences. In this spirit, the eighteenth-century German writer Johann Wolfgang von Goethe liked to talk about the beauty of double-entry book keeping. He was directing attention away from what is coming in or being spent, and onto the method of recording. The spiritual advantage of this apparently tedious task is that it permits accuracy. Virgil was writing as a man absolutely at the centre of his educated culture – he carried a great deal of glamour and emotional, moral weight. And he uses that position in his writings to draw our attention to what might look like minor practical matters – what to do when it rains, for instance (number your sacks of grain, weave baskets, mend the plough, grind corn). He mixes very practical instruction with discussion of the gods and the meaning of life. The small matters join up with the great. So that in undertaking apparently minor tasks one can see how and why one is contributing to something genuinely good. It stops feeling futile.

We might tend to suppose that by isolating a chore and cutting it from our lives we make it more manageable. That, I think, is the meaning of my father's shut-up desk. The annoying, tedious, uncomfortable tasks can be sealed off – so that they don't contaminate the rest of one's existence. Virgil and Goethe take the opposite view. They look at mundane, tricky, continuous activities and bring them towards the centre of one's self-conception.

In one of the poems Virgil is discussing the rhythm of work. It's autumn:

> A farmer's work proceeds in
> Cycles, as the shuttling year returns in its own track.
> And now, the time when a vineyard puts off its reluctant leaves
> And a bitter north wind has blown away the pride of the woodland,
> Even now the countryman actively pushes on to the coming
> Year and its tasks; attacking the naked vine with a curved
> Pruning-knife, he shears and trims it into shape.
> Be the first to dig the land, the first to wheel off the prunings

> *For the bonfire, the first to bring your vine-pole under cover;*
> *But the last to gather the vintage . . .*
> *It makes for hard work.*

Nothing that he says makes the tasks he writes about any less difficult. What he is doing is dignifying labour by connecting it up to the grander aspects of existence. He writes of mythology and the seasons and of local religion, he describes the wisdom and foresight of the good farmer, the devotion to all the necessary steps in cultivating the soil.

There is a crucial parallel here with the constant labour of maintaining financial order. One could project an updated Virgil who tells us of the rhythm of the financial year . . . *Now the last swallows are departing, and the first gales of winter shake your roof, now is the time for sorting through your bank statements and receipts. On your way home from work look in at a junk shop and buy two wooden boxes large enough to hold A4 sheets of paper. And take yourself also, as the sun is setting, to a stationery supplier and get yourself a quantity of manila folders, the colour of hope. Dine early and lay all the pieces of paper before you on the carpet. Divide them, as the Gods divide the just from the unjust, into two piles. Arrange them by date. Work slowly. And when you are done, pour a libation to Apollo, who loves clarity and order. On the second night, consecrate your mind to calculation. On the third, devote yourself to the filling of forms. In this way you spread your work evenly across the season.*

Virgil dignifies instruction – he assumes that you are an educated, interesting, thoughtful, sensitive (that is, normal) person. And he approaches his task not as someone scolding us, or bothering us into compliance, but as a poet and a philosopher.

Ultimately, one is cultivating an art – one of the minor political arts, the art of domestic finance. By saying that it is an art, one is getting at the idea that there are multiple motives and rewards, which are integrated. There is an *aesthetics* of order – a physical beauty that is connected to neatness and clarity – like the beauty of the periodic table, or the elegance of a mathematical equation, or the rightness of a note in a sonata. It is a classical beauty.

I believe it is extremely important to separate the task of organizing from the task of confronting – because these are psychologically very different activities. You must undertake the ordering as if you were arranging a collection of shells, or postcards, or somebody else's papers. As for confronting, I believe the best method is to do this gradually, in stages. It is just not possible to solve everything at once. It simply won't happen. But this is akin to other tasks – that of learning a language or a musical instrument or a sport. There is a danger of looking at the whole too soon and too intently. It petrifies one's efforts and humiliates one's beginning achievements.

In his writings Virgil is trying to close the gap between what we *have* to do and what we admire ourselves *for* doing. He casts the mantle of cultural glamour and charm over ordinary activity – so that these activities feel more enticing, more like activities you'd want to be associated with. This is the mark of a good and helpful culture – it helps us *enjoy* what it is important and good for us to *do*.

# VI. How to Make Money and be a Good Person at the Same Time

# 1. Having and Doing

Right at the start of this book I suggested that one of the typical worries we have about money is that it is like a 'virus' (see page 10). This is a general, social anxiety. But it can be manifested in the form of a very personal fear: *unless I sell my soul I won't be able to make enough money to meet my needs.* When I ask myself how much money I need in order to live a flourishing life (rather than just get by) the figures are alarmingly big. How can I get that much money?

Put it another way: if I follow my heart's desire, when it comes to work, I fear that I won't be able to make enough money to live the kind of life I think I should.

A version of this worry forms itself in the minds of fond parents listening to their children's hopes about adult existence. The traditional experience goes something like this:

SEVEN-YEAR-OLD: I'm going to have five Land Rovers and a helicopter and two swimming pools and a huge trampoline and . . .

PARENT: That's lovely. And how are you going to afford all that? Are you going to have a job?

SEVEN-YEAR-OLD: Yes, I'm going to drive the school bus.

This scenario arises from the child's innocence. As yet, they have no idea of the connection between what you do and what monetary reward you get. The seven-year-old assumption is that the more fun an activity is, the more good things flow from it. The essence of this hope is: 'I want to get massively rewarded for having a nice time being myself.' That's why, amongst school children, being a sports star or a supermodel are the most popular 'career' options. The desire itself is natural. Unfortunately, success in these fields requires extremely high levels of natural skill or luck.

And there is a more worldly version of this parent–child scenario, which brings worries of another kind:

SEVEN-YEAR-OLD: I'm going to be an estate agent.

PARENT: Why?

SEVEN-YEAR-OLD: Because they make the most money.

Further questioning reveals that the child's choice is based on a simple assumption about size: the bigger the thing you sell, the more money you must make. It is also a choice driven by the belief that money equals happiness. And one realizes that the child has only reluctantly come to the conclusion that being a bank robber, though beautifully lucrative, is too risky. But there is a certain pathos, too, in the innocent belief that all that matters in a working life is how much money you make.

These childhood episodes are important because they imagine a world that is fundamentally simpler than we know ours to be.

In these worlds you only have to solve one problem. Do what you like doing – and you will be rich; get paid well – and the soul will be fulfilled.

What we face in reality is the need to solve two problems at the same time. We need to make enough money (to meet our real needs) and we need to do things that help to make sense of who we are and meet our deep longing for meaning and to contribute to the collective good. You can escape – it's true – by not caring about meaning and the collective good. And you can escape by not caring about having much money. But a lot of people care about both.

There are quite profound reasons why we should care simultaneously about having and doing. Both are connected to flourishing.

What we do with our lives is obviously central to who we are. What we expend our mental energy on, what we put our emotional resources into, where we deploy courage or daring or prudence or commitment: these are major parts of existence and are inevitably much connected with work and earning money. And we need these parts of existence in order to find proper application in activities that *deserve* our best efforts. We don't want to reserve our central capacities for the margins and weekends of life.

Equally, as I have argued, to consider what one needs money *for* is not frivolous. The opportunities and possessions money affords us are, at least sometimes, very important to us.

Perhaps unconsciously, we often have a picture of the relationship between satisfaction and earning that looks like this:

Think of the hedge-fund manager who reaps vast rewards for doing something that seems to have no intrinsic merit. Or consider the early-years teacher who helps a shy child feel more confident but is very modestly paid for such important and good work.

For what it's worth, in the ideal, utopian economy, the relationship would look like this:

At an individual level, one is trying to find a way of making this happen in one's own life. But because intrinsic worth is not just what is good for me, but what is *actually* good, this is a public service as well. It's not greedy to want to make quite a lot of money – if you want to make it as a reward for doing things that are genuinely good for other people.

When I first moved to London in the late 1980s everyone seemed to be making money – except me. I had recently finished a university degree in philosophy. I didn't know what to do with my life. I shared a tiny room (8 feet by 5) with my cousin in a flat in a run-down area south of the river. I had some casual work as a waiter – the impatience of customers when I was doing my best, and when the delay in the arrival of their food had nothing at all to do with me, made me weep with humiliated rage.

I began a research degree, which put me further in debt. After an evening seminar we'd go out for beers. But this often meant I had to walk home, having spent my tube fare, through miles of grim urban decay. My friend Chris, who was doing brilliantly in his researches on Nietzsche, got a part-time job filling shelves at Harrods. He reported his brother's wry remark: 'All that insight into the meaning of life and here you are making sure the jam labels are facing outwards.' He was, rather brutally, pointing out that certain very real merits don't join up easily with the demands of the economy. Chris wanted more money. But he didn't just want that. He also wanted to live in a world in which there would be a better outlet – a better market, you might say – for his talents.

There is a general worry here that 'capitalism' is a damaged system, but one that we are probably stuck with for a very long time.

It often looks quite cruel and yet there is no clear path out of it. This breeds pervasive gloom. So I want to look at some ways in which we might come to feel a bit more hopeful about the big picture.

The personal and general worries are connected. Both look at the same problem: it seems too difficult to combine flourishing financially and being a good person. We worry that we can't have both.

# 2. What Rex Got Wrong and Other Lessons

The great task is to understand how the pursuit of profit, individually and collectively, can be combined with the serious pursuit of higher worth. Is it possible to make money by meeting the higher needs of humanity?

The answer to this question lies in considering some of the causes of profit and translating them from their familiar use in meeting basic and middle-order needs and understanding how they might apply in addressing the deeper needs of the soul.

Incidentally, paying attention to the causes of profit helps demystify the ways in which money is made. There's often a residual suspicion that wealth is accumulated by exploitation, that money is made by some people because, in effect, they take money away from others. (This belief is enshrined in the myth that wealth is a cause of poverty.)

To address this, we can ask ourselves the following questions: What are the examples of money-making that speak to your soul? What is actually going on in those cases?

By way of illustration, here are four examples from my collection.

## i. The Lesson of the Chance Card

In the version of Monopoly that we play, there's a Chance card that reads 'You buy a watercolour at Camden market and sell it for a huge profit. Collect £200,000.' The card reflects one of the most basic ideas about making money.

At the stall, surrounded by bric-a-brac, shorn of the artist's name and without a frame, the little piece of coloured paper lacks the obvious markers of desirability and value. But the trained eye can recognize the primary markers of financial worth – the style of a particular hand; quality of execution. Elegantly mounted and framed, with a plaque announcing a famous name, in a hushed and opulent gallery in Mayfair, anyone can see that it is going to command a high price.

So one relevant virtue is lack of prejudice – you don't judge things according to the environment, but as they are, in and of themselves. This goes against the grain of many social habits. Money is then made by repositioning that object with the relevant secondary markers of value.

The other virtue, here, is a grasp of what the right context would be. What is it that you need to do with the object in order to make its worth obvious to more people? In the gallery example the answer to this question has already been worked out. (Of course, this process finds its moral opposite in charlatanism, in which the secondary markers of value are deployed in the absence of real worth.)

Spot the priceless treasure.

## ii. What Rex Got Wrong

There's an episode in Evelyn Waugh's *Brideshead Revisited* in which the central character, Charles, is living in Paris and goes out to dinner with Rex Mottram – a crude, grasping financial adventurer and Member of Parliament.

Rex is paying and they go to Charles's favourite restaurant. In a quiet way, it is perfect. Rex likes the food, but then thinks of how much more profitable the place could be 'if someone were really to take it in hand'. We know what that would mean. Its real virtues would be lost; it would become ostentatious and garish; the prices would be ratcheted up; it would pander to the demands of gossip and fashion. Charles is disgusted. And so one is tempted to cheer for Charles and feel that commercialization is the enemy and that it belongs to odious, insensitive people like Rex. The fear is that by commercializing something you have to cheapen and degrade it. What was gracious and intimate becomes a crass mass-market entity. And – obviously – this is a real danger.

But there is another path we could take. As it is, the restaurant is doing many things extremely well. And it is, clearly, much better than many other places. So, the person who is sympathetic to Charles should want there to be more such restaurants. They should want that kind of accomplishment to be normal, rather than rare. But if we ask why it is rare, the answer will be something like this: not many people know how to make it happen. Somewhere in the background is the knowledge of how to make this particular restaurant so fine – how to make it subtle and beautiful, how to design a menu and maintain a high pitch of quality, how to create an atmosphere that invites people to be elegant, thoughtful versions of themselves.

And we should want that kind of knowledge to be widespread and to have more sway in the world. The process of commercialization is the process of working out how those genuinely good qualities can be brought to fruition in more places. How could that kind of intelligence guide the management of a bar or a hotel, for instance? For me the *Brideshead* example is important because, for a long time, it gripped my imagination. I thought of commercialization as belonging to the Rexes of the world. So I never asked myself how the things that I cared about could compete effectively in the world. Without realizing it, I adopted a tragic cast of mind. I assumed that profit was the enemy – and that was to concede power and consequence to all that I disliked.

Unconsciously I assumed that what was good could not also be profitable: the finest films would lose money; the noblest poetry wouldn't sell. Quality and meaningfulness therefore required government subsidy in order to exist. I hoped that politicians would intervene in the marketplace and ensure a safe, uncompetitive zone for beauty and seriousness. Later I came to see that politics is a poor mechanism for bringing this about. Politics reflects the existing dominant concerns of a society, the minds of ambitious politicians have to be focused on winning elections – and that means addressing the concerns of carefully targeted bands of voters in swing constituencies. In a grand sense, the flourishing of beauty, goodness and truth is the central political concern – which is to say that it is a great collective task. But the real constraints of the political process mean that governments will not be the powerful angels of these ideals. So those who wish to see the flourishing of such matters have to engage with the marketplaces in which a culture is enacted. And commercialization is the name of that engagement.

## iii. The Lesson of the Landmark Trust

We should take inspiration from the Landmark Trust, which was established in the UK in the 1980s and now also operates in France, Italy and the US. The starting point was a desire to save and preserve interesting, beautiful buildings that would otherwise fall into ruin or be demolished. They were, typically, not of such outstanding historical and architectural merit as to justify the intervention of the state, which would preserve them as part of the national heritage. The aim, instead, was to commercialize these buildings: that is, turn them into experiences that could be sold at a sufficiently high price to cover their upkeep.

In this case the thing being sold – the experience of holidaying in one of these places – is very fine. They are decorated and furnished in a way that is both fairly simple and really refined. The fear would be that by packaging and selling holidays, the integrity and charm of these buildings would be sacrificed. Instead, the trust was so intelligently managed that the real worth of the buildings was grasped, and *that* is what is on offer. They have found a way of making the good flourish in the marketplace.

The closely related term 'commodification' is also often used in a hostile, negative spirit, indicating a process that we should lament. But really what we should resist is poor-quality commodification. Commodification is simply the process of translating an unsaleable

Commodification and the pursuit of profit created this.

experience or kind of object into a form in which it can be quantified and graded in standard ways, and traded. When the city of Edinburgh expanded into the New Town, from about 1785 to 1825, building plots and house designs were 'commodified'. You could purchase an interest in a quantity of land with the right to build a house of a specific, closely defined grade. And these interests could be divided up and traded. But in that case, commodification did not lead to the spiritual corruption of the nation or to the sullying of beauty by trade. On the contrary it was the economic base which enabled the construction of some of the loveliest terraces, squares and crescents in the world.

The standard grading of buildings in this case was sensitive to – in fact a grading of – extremely fine ideas about urban architecture. Perhaps the planners were historically very lucky: grading and standardization was in the hands of exceptionally civilized public servants, who combined elegant taste with a flair for finance.

What goes wrong with commodification is not that there is standardization of grades of quality, or a market in trading quantities of something. What goes wrong is that the grades and the quantities do not reflect our best understanding of the value of what is at stake. A standardized hotel room, for instance, typically lacks soul. But that's because it standardizes the soulless aspects of accommodation. With greater insight and skill we could standardize homeliness and intimacy.

## iv. The Lesson of Henry Ford

'Industrialization' is the name we give to the process by which work that was once undertaken by many small independent providers is reorganized so as to enable economies of scale. The classic sequence of industrialization was followed in the early days of car manufacture. At first, many small companies each made a few vehicles. It was Henry Ford who reorganized production so that a large number of cars could be made more efficiently and hence sold much more cheaply.

Romantically we tend to be prejudiced in favour of small operations. And we think of industrialization as a slightly dreary fact of economic necessity rather than something to be sought in connection with our nobler aspirations. We assume it is acceptable for car manufacturing but not for inter-personal relationships.

Take, for instance, psychotherapy. At present there are a great many small-scale producers. There are many different schools of psychotherapy, quite variable in quality, each with their own training programme. The service is run out of people's homes, or suites of consulting rooms. The public image of psychotherapy is of a slightly mysterious process of uncertain utility. Therapists are associated with eccentric habits of dress and conduct. The more organized part of the profession is connected to medicine and deals (as medicine tends to) only with extreme problems. Psychotherapy is expensive, a bit embarrassing, slow and unreliable.

And yet, considered from a distance, psychotherapy is an obviously important human activity. The basic premise is that a great many people suffer from troubles of the inner life. We mess up our relationships; we feel sad about our lives; we sabotage our hopes and feel unproductively angry. 'Quiet desperation' and 'life leaking away' are phrases that speak to our common condition. We can function and get by, but wish for much more than this. And the guiding principle of psychotherapy is that real help can be provided. If we can find the right way of addressing our inner lives then these troubles can be relieved. We can sustain more satisfying relationships, make better choices about the direction of our lives and make more constructive use of our capacities.

One could apply the approach of Henry Ford (and the Model-T Ford) to the needs of inner life. Better research and training could be provided for psychotherapists if there were a more secure career path. The public perception could be improved if there were the resources to advertise, to make issues stick in common culture, if offices were more elegant and the status and character of therapists more refined. And yes, more money could be made. It's a matter of scale and organization. This is the wisdom of industrialization.

## v. The Lesson of Aristotle

At the start of the *Nicomachean Ethics*, Aristotle sets forth the basic relationship of means and ends. 'Every art and every investigation, and similarly every action and choice is considered to aim at some good.' Hence, you cannot properly understand an activity, or an investigation, until you know what good it aims at.

We need to understand the end, so that we can properly grasp what the means should be.

Very often activities are organized in more than one stage. Aristotle explains this with a now quaint example – but, of course, he was talking about a big technology industry of his time. 'A skill in making bridles or any other part of a horse's trappings comes under horsemanship, while this and every other kind of military action comes under military science.' And military science itself falls under politics: the wider and more important science of good societies.

The logic of the argument is clear: a good bridle is one that enables better control of a horse, in terms of what people want or need to do with horses. But horsemanship is itself – in one major way – subject to the art of generalship. Which is to say that the point, in this context, of being good at governing a horse is to be able to participate effectively in military activities. But it is not the horseman who defines 'effective' here. It is the art of generalship that identifies what is needed from the cavalry. But generalship is itself subject to the arts of politics. That is, the point of fighting is only to obtain further ends, and those further ends are not skill in fighting battles, but the security and flourishing of a state – and that does not belong under generalship but under politics.

What this boils down to is this: at each stage you have to ask what is the good that is being served? What do we need this thing to be like if it is to be really helpful and important to us?

It's crucial that Aristotle thinks of the 'end' or goal as a good. What good does the activity or investigation aim at? That's why this discussion is central to ethics, which seeks knowledge of the good. And it is why questions of money are always questions of ethics.

Aristotle is elaborating an issue that has great significance for human undertakings. It's been co-opted into business thinking under the dry name of 'vertical integration', in which different businesses simultaneously supply various components for one over-arching owner. But really the idea comes from Aristotle – though in his model everyone is working not for some tycoon but for a higher ideal.

One area that desperately needs this type of vertical integration is art. At present, people define themselves as being 'interested in art'. Then they go to art school, develop their ideas and later seek exhibitions. Galleries seek saleable work and try to promote artists. Collectors follow their own inclinations and, for whatever reasons they may have, make the careers of certain artists by buying their work. At some point, public institutions endorse and eventually canonize a few artists as highly important. Along the way there are various publicity mechanisms – reviews in newspapers, interviews in magazines, and so on. Somewhere in the background there are debates about the nature and value of art.

But in comparison with Aristotle's model this is a chaotic system. Little attention is given to the underlying issue: what good does art actually serve, and how can we maximize the provision of that good? If these questions were answered, galleries and art schools would have a defined target, which could in turn inform the recruitment of people to those art schools.

What follows from such instances and analyses? I'm not really trying to give guidance in money-making schemes. After all, this isn't a how-to guide on making money. One can so easily feel crushed by the success of others that it's really helpful to keep in mind a crucial distinction that the examples point to. Money *can* be made in really good ways. So we should always be asking *how* people made their money – not just *how much* they happen to have. When wealth is made by really serving the best interests of humanity, then the people who make money this way are our friends – in imagination, I mean. So you don't have to be anti-money to be critical of many of the sources of wealth.

This speaks to quite a big theme in life – but one that, I feel, doesn't get enough attention. It's to do with how we position ourselves in relation to the economic successes and failures of others. I have so many social conversations in which people are pro- or anti-money. But I've found that making case studies like those above gives me a feeling of inner solidity. I know why and when I admire wealth creation. And that leaves me free to be critical when necessary, without feeling that I'm just bitter.

There's another benefit I'd like to mention as well. At work, I'm involved in thinking about how academic departments, which see themselves as non-commercial, can increase their incomes. Many of my colleagues see this as a miserable climbdown. But the case studies point to ways in which reaching a market and seeking profit are capable of being noble activities. This helps refocus the imagination. We're not having to swallow the advice of a university equivalent of Rex Mottram; we're trying to be a bit more like the Landmark Trust.

It's not naive to think that you can pursue profit and do something inherently good at the same time. It's just tricky – but that's fine, work is about solving tricky problems.

# VII. My Place in the Big Picture

# 1. The Problems of the Rich

How well off – or poor – you feel usually depends on who else you are thinking about. Walking across New York's Upper East Side makes me feel poverty-stricken, while it can be oddly therapeutic to drive through an impoverished suburb or neighbourhood. That's because we tend to reframe our thoughts about ourselves according to the current environment.

Because the desire for wealth is almost universal, and almost always frustrated, it is extremely important for us, as individuals and collectively, to keep at the front of our minds the problems and troubles of the rich.

We tend not to do this because we think 'Why should I feel sorry for them?' But the point isn't to do moral justice to those individuals. The point is to equip oneself for a life of not being rich, but also of not longing fruitlessly to be so.

## i. The problems of inheritance

Inherited wealth comes with the wrong strings attached: 'I gave you this; even from beyond the grave I control your life, and you must judge your existence according to my standards; I own your soul', a kind of 'ancestor envy'. The bar of what counts as success is set extremely high.

The rich-by-inheritance are prone to guilt. The question 'why me?' cannot fail to arise in a thoughtful mind (and not having a thoughtful mind is a trouble, too – though of a different kind). There is no straightforward answer; it's pure luck that this person happened to be conceived by their parents – they have not 'earned' their wealth, so they feel they lack a moral right to it.

These people are the natural targets of envy. They are continually confronted by people who feel 'You have it easy while the rest of us have to slave away.' The voice of envy says to the great inheritor: 'I hate you; I want what you have; you shouldn't have it; I should have it; you must feel anguish and guilt, but if I had what you have I would be happy.' And to know that that's what people feel about you must be extremely disconcerting.

So, what's the answer here? How should someone who has inherited a fair bit of money feel about it?

1. Many good things are distributed unequally and for no humane reason: good looks; sporting prowess; good health; an even temperament; mental appetite and ability; easy normality, sociability and wit; wise, warm parents . . . Economic inheritance is just one thing amongst many – it isn't a special case.

2. Because you yourself were not involved in awarding your inheritance, you should try not to feel any superstitious sense of endorsement or entitlement.

3. You won't be judged fairly by other people. But that is a normal part of life; not something that happens purely because of inheritance. It is a normal feature of the world that applies to inheritance, because it applies to everything.

## ii. The problem of envy

One should also note that wealth does not protect people from feeling envy. There's a strangely exciting entry in the diary of Chips Channon, a rich American socialite in London in the 1930s. He lived in an exquisitely beautiful house, gave opulent dinner parties and lived what looks – from the outside – like the most carefree and charming life.

He mentions staying at an overwhelmingly majestic house, Mentmore Towers, belonging to the Rothschilds: 'I am, I fear, sick with envy.' (Suffering a hangover, he acted out his hostility, smashing the gilded chamber pot that had been made for the ablutions of the Emperor Napoleon.)

The point is a simple one: despite everything he had, Channon was still prey to desperate envy. The lesson, here, is that money does not liberate people in the way that we assume it must. If one can internalize this lesson and have it at the front of one's mind it operates like a psychological safety harness. *They* suffer. Therefore their lot is not a solution to my problems.

The man who lived here . . .

. . . felt sick with envy when he stayed here.

## iii. The problem of dissipation

Money in large quantities takes away barriers to action. The person with secure riches can do what they want. And – horrible though this fact is – this is usually the road to unhappiness. There is a very imperfect relationship between desire and flourishing. Desire aims at pleasure. Whereas the achievement of a good life depends upon the good we create. And the opportunity to follow whatever desire one might happen to have is the enemy of the effort, concentration, devotion, patience and self-sacrifice that are necessary if we are to achieve worthwhile ends.

The person who can afford to go out every day to lunch and drink two bottles of champagne has to refrain from doing so, if they are to have a decent life. So every day they have to fight off a temptation. Immediately the idea of lunch and champagne feels very appealing. But it leads nowhere. Every day they could jump in a plane and go off somewhere else: but to what purpose? *I'll sleep in Venice tonight. No, Paris is very nice, perhaps I should go there?* But nothing is ever enough. *My private jet is too small. My island is the wrong shape. I want a happy family and twenty-three mistresses. If I dislike someone I want to destroy them, and I can. The government wants to take away my money. I don't trust my lawyers and my financial advisers: they are only interested in what they can get out of me.*

## iv. The problem of underachievement

We think of the rich – at least those who have made their money themselves – as high achievers. But this isn't quite right. Making money is only the first step.

Historically, wealth has been deployed in some really magnificent ways. And really high achievement has to be assessed in comparison with what others have *done* with their money. A rich man made this:

What imaginative and economic powers combined to raise this edifice?

This library, now a reading room, has stood the test of time and has been an inspiration – a symbol of the union of grace and wisdom – to huge numbers of people. It required money, of course. But it took a lot more than that. Many people have more than enough cash to equal the achievement. But they don't compete in this league. They underachieve, relative to their resources. Today's equivalent might not look physically so grand. But it should have grandeur of another kind. Of course there are stellar examples of philanthropy. And that's a trouble for the rich. They really should rise to the heights of those philanthropic examples – but often they know they don't.

The lesson here isn't that we should pity the rich. Instead we are trying to cultivate something that would have appealed to Jane Austen: our own dignity.

Perhaps the most famous scene in *Pride and Prejudice* is when Elizabeth Bennet turns down Mr Darcy's first offer of marriage. In refusing him, she catalogues the troubles of the rich. He is proud, in a selfish way; he thinks he can get whatever he wants; he looks down on her family (who deserve tenderness); and he thinks he's doing her a great favour by overlooking, despite his best judgement, the difference in their social levels. Elizabeth is brilliantly retaining her own dignity by seeing what is going wrong with Darcy. The problem is never his wealth, as such. She wouldn't dream of doing him down simply for having a lot of money.

# 2. The Virtues of Poverty

There are unexpected lessons to be learned from those who have managed to find fulfilment without money. Because the fear of poverty is so great and so widespread, we should educate ourselves as individuals and collectively to grasp the potential good of poverty. This is not meant as a way of ignoring the sufferings of poverty – rather, it's a response to our own ceaseless anxiety. It would be liberating to be a bit less afraid.

What can be good about poverty, and is there anything we can learn from it, without necessarily undergoing the experience of being poor? This sounds bizarre, but in the past people have often esteemed poverty – not starvation, humiliation or anxiety, but indifference to possessions and avoidance of ownership. St Francis of Assisi, for example, thought that voluntary poverty was a positive good. 'St Francis ... did, above all things, execrate money', writes one of the authors of *The Mirror of Perfection*, the thirteenth-century account of the saint's life. A remarkable episode is recorded in this volume. One day a pilgrim came into the church where Francis was staying and left, as a pious offering, a golden coin upon the altar. One of the monks threw the coin out of the window. But that was not enough for St Francis. 'He bade him lift the money with his mouth and put it on the dung of an ass. And all they that did see and hear were filled with very great fear, and from that time forth did despise money more than the dung of an ass ...'

This attitude of intense hatred of money derives from a complete view of life. Material possessions and prestige are regarded not only as unimportant but as terribly dangerous: they are seen as inherently corrupting.

So what benefits might we derive from this sort of asceticism?

1. Freedom from obsession, and from being preoccupied with getting and spending. But this requires an account of what else you should be giving your attention to. St Francis loved poverty because he loved something else: nature and simplicity. He wanted to give his whole mind to being part of the natural order, which he thought of as God's creation. Sunlight, a bird, a flower were his models of ideal being. The love of such things is not manifest as ownership.

2. Finer perception: by being distanced from the noise and striving of the great world one can see people and things as they really are. There are some fine observations in Dr Johnson's early poem 'London', written when he was very poor: he notes that *because* men like to draw smoke inside themselves, there are buildings where clay is turned into tubes (pipes) and fields where weeds are grown; and because many people think well of themselves if they attach sparkly objects to their heads (he's talking about earrings) others spend their lives digging in the ground looking for things that reflect light to an uncommon degree (diamonds), while others have little booths in which they

exchange these things for lumps of metal (gold). He sees the underlying strangeness of much of the activity of the world. And it is this perception, established when he was poor, that fitted him to be such a powerful thinker.

3. Independence: if you do not care for the things that other people want your motives are true. The ancient Romans loved the story of Cincinnatus who, despite being a great soldier, lived a life of utter simplicity, ploughing the fields himself and eating plain bread. At a time of national insecurity he was given emergency powers as a temporary dictator. Having defeated the enemy he was in a position to attain great wealth. He returned, however, to his frugal life. The Romans regarded him as a model of the incorruptible man, because there was nothing other people could offer him that would deflect him from what he thought to be right. He could not be bought. And therefore he could be trusted with unrestricted power.

What, if anything, can one learn from such examples? To be sure, just being poor is no guarantee that any of these benefits will accrue: they don't attach themselves automatically where there is an absence of cash. Rather they depend upon a voluntary condition: a willingness to not have the things that most people do want. They come from not being afraid of lack of money. They depend, positively, on something else: inner security. Cincinnatus could go without any of the rewards that were supposed to be the whole point of success, because his attention was elsewhere. He had, one might say, an inner wealth that made external wealth unimportant to him. And that, of course, is precisely what is usually not the case in poverty. It's the same with Dr Johnson and St Francis. In each case the capacity to deal well with poverty depended upon having an entirely different kind of internal resource, a source of dignity that could not be touched by money.

The three men we are looking at chose to be frugal – they had the option of getting more money. They had a choice that many people don't have. They had a physical experience of poverty; but the mental experience was quite different.

The point, here, isn't that it is good to be poor. These examples are of very unusual men. The lesson they point to is that people become less concerned about money the more they are devoted to something else. Personally, I want to learn this lesson a *little*, and see what it tells us about relationships to money. But it's a lesson that takes us to the very centre of money worries and what to do about them; it links up with everything we've been talking about in this book.

# 3. The Intimate Relationship with Money

As I was saying at the very start, money *worries* aren't like money *troubles*. Worries are to do with imagination and emotion. They involve how we compare ourselves with others, the dangers (and occasional benefits) of envy, how we understand our needs, what we care about and why, how we deal with the long term versus the short term.

Thinking about the problems of the rich and the (ideal) virtues of poverty allows us to see something crucial about relationships to money.

The quality of a relationship depends on what you bring and on what the other party (in this case money) brings. It's possible to have a great relationship with an apparently unpromising thing (poverty) if you bring a huge set of wonderful resources to the encounter. And if you bring very little, it doesn't matter how much the thing (riches) promises, because you can't do anything good with it.

The quality of the relationship isn't a matter of sheer intensity. In Balzac's *Old Goriot* there's a fabulous description of an old man in an attic fingering his little pile of gold. He caresses the coins, he gloats over them. It's almost like an erotic encounter. But this is a terrible relationship. He's really only deploying a very small part of himself – his greed for possession. It's all-consuming, but leaves out almost everything that should go into a good relationship: self-knowledge, wisdom, generosity, kindness, appetite for life and for new experience.

Or consider again Cincinnatus, who could have had the wealth of Rome in his hands, but instead chose to farm his fields. Not because he was denying himself, or because he thought he would be praised for it, but because – for him – that was the more enjoyable pursuit. We may not have the choice between the two, as he did, but there is pleasure to be found in simple things, once we stop resenting the fact that they are not grander. Cincinnatus could put the best of himself into his farming.

Money *troubles* are really just about money – not about the relationship. If I have a heap of debts and bills and no money I'm in real trouble; and it doesn't matter how interesting or mature my view of life is, or how imaginative I am, or how beautiful my taste. None of those fine qualities will help. I've either got to find more cash, or restructure, or go under.

Our money *worries* are almost all about the relationship. They are largely about what is going on in our minds. And the solution – the way to worry less about money – turns out to be about improving what we as individuals bring to the relationship. We need to look at our own contribution. We need to become more imaginative, more patient, more attentive to the lessons of our own experience, more serious about the things we most care for, more canny, more independent in our judgements. But most importantly, we have to figure out what we actually need.

I know at first sight this seems strange. Surely, we think, worrying less about money must be to do with getting more money or coping with having less than we'd like. But however obvious this seems it can't be quite right. One's relationship with money is only in part about money – it's mainly about other things. And so we have to

The civilized ideal: elegance and devotion to work. Johann Joseph Schmeller,
*Goethe in His Study Dictating to His Secretary John*, 1831.

make a surprising, but vital, leap of understanding. We have to look into ourselves and think what money means to us.

My ideal representative of the refusal to worry too much about money is Johann Wolfgang von Goethe. From his many writings about his own experiences, we know he was determined to get well paid for his work. He came from a well-off background but sought independence. He switched careers, from law to government adviser so as to be able to earn more (which made sense then; today the trajectory might be in the opposite direction). He coped with serious setbacks. His first novel was extremely popular but he made no money from it because of inadequate copyright laws. Later, he negotiated better contracts. He was very competent in financial matters and kept meticulous records of his income and expenditure. He liked what money could buy – including, as we see on the previous page, a stylish house-coat (his study had no heating). But for all this, money and money worries did not dominate his inner life. He wrote with astonishing sensitivity about love and beauty. He was completely realistic and pragmatic when it came to money but this did not lead him to neglect the worth of exploring bigger, more important concepts in life.

He's a helpful sort of hero to have in mind because he had a very good relationship with money. He struck the right balance between caring about making money and focusing on the other things that were really important to him.

Of course, like all heroes, he's also pleasingly distant, historically, geographically and ideologically far enough away from us that we can see his achievements in sharper relief. But that only gives us a clearer target at which to aim.

# Homework

I've found help in thinking about money in many places, some of them a bit surprising at first sight. I'd recommend any of the books mentioned below. And not only for what they say about money.

## I. Introduction

My thinking about worries – as opposed to troubles – was inspired by a radio talk by Adam Phillips. He spoke insightfully about what we are doing when we worry, using the example of a dog 'worrying' a bone.

## II. Thinking About Money

### 1. What are Money Worries Really About?

The Western philosophical tradition begins with Socrates getting people to ask questions where traditionally they wouldn't think there was a question to be asked. He took things his contemporaries admired, such as courage, and got them to ask seriously: 'but what do I mean by "courage"?' The best example of this approach is Plato's *Republic*, in which Socrates leads a discussion on the question 'what is justice?' Socrates is the great patron of the idea that we make progress in thinking only when we focus on asking the right questions.

## 2. A Good Relationship with Money

My general approach to relationships is inspired by Donald Winnicott. He took the view that we are essentially relationship-forming creatures – and that our relationships to ideas and objects, including money, turn out to have much in common with our more familiar relationships to people. Thus one could speak of a child 'making friends' with maths and see the role of a maths teacher as (ideally) the enabler of such a friendship. *Playing and Reality* is a good introduction to his work.

# III. The Secret Meaning of Money

## 1. When Money is Not Money

The question of what money is in someone's mind is finely explored in *The Forsyte Saga*, written by John Galsworthy and wonderfully adapted for television in 1967. For the central character, Soames Forsyte, money means goodness and desirability. He is long blind to the growing problems of his first marriage, because it is inconceivable to him that his wife could be unhappy with him, given how much money he makes. It's not that he thinks she is greedy for money. He knows she wants love. But he thinks that he really is giving her love by giving her money, because in his imagination money and love are the same thing.

Dickens is also very good on this topic. In *Bleak House* money is confused with justice and in *Little Dorrit* with dignity – in both cases with disastrous consequences.

## 2. How to Strip Off

The process of analysing one's unconscious attitudes to money is loosely derived from Freud. He takes the view that we unconsciously connect things that, in reality, are quite separate – thus damaging our capacity to behave appropriately. A good place to start is Freud's *Outline of Psychoanalysis*.

## 3. What is Money?

There is a very readable discussion of the definition of money in the first chapter of *The Ascent of Money* by Niall Ferguson.

# IV. Money and the Good Life

## 1. Money as an Ingredient

A stimulating and wise guide to Aristotle's economics can be found in *The Political Thought of Plato and Aristotle* by Sir Ernest Barker, first published in 1906. He explains Aristotle's idea that money is just a resource (like a heap of building materials) that can be used well or badly. But money itself tells us nothing about how to do this – no more than a pile of bricks shows you how to construct a beautiful house.

Dickens, again, is a brilliant exponent of the 'ingredient' approach to money. Some of his most noble characters, such as Mr Brownlow in *Oliver Twist*, are as well off as some of his greatest villains, like Mr Gradgrind in *Hard Times*. It's not money in itself that makes the difference.

## 2. Jane Austen's Theory of Marriage

Jane Austen's *Sense and Sensibility* is a wonderful love story, of course; at the same time it is a careful attempt to distinguish between financial prudence and self-indulgence. In fact, all her novels have double economic themes. On the one hand, having enough money is taken very seriously as a necessary condition of happy marriage and either the heroine or the hero has to face this problem. In *Persuasion*, for instance, Captain Wentworth has to make his fortune in the chances of war before he is able to get together with Anne, his true love. On the other hand, Jane Austen is always keen to show us people who have plenty of money yet fail in their lives, such as the Crawfords in *Mansfield Park*.

## 3. Envy as Education

A classic statement of how we should use envy to educate ourselves can be found in the final chapter of Alain de Botton's book *The Consolations of Philosophy*.

# V. Creating Order

## 1. Need versus Want

On the hierarchy of needs the classic statements come from Maslow's 1943 paper 'A Theory of Human Motivation'.

## 2. How Much Money Do I Need?

There is a witty analysis of how much money a couple needs to live on in the TV comedy classic *The Good Life*, which had its first series in 1975.

## 3. Price versus Value

Art critic John Ruskin's strangely titled *Muneris Pulvera* of 1871 opens with a magnificent attempt to reconnect price and value. Despite being written so long ago, it remains the clearest and most ambitious statement of the need for a value-based economy. Ruskin argues that money is *the potential possession of good things*. Actual possession of genuinely good things constitutes wealth. But, sadly, money also enables the possession of harmful and worthless things – a condition he calls *illth*. He argues that the price of a product should be determined by how much good effort of hand or brain was required to make it, rather than by the level of demand.

### 4. Longing and Fear

I recommend C. Day Lewis's translation of Virgil's *The Georgics*.

## VI. How to Make Money and be a Good Person at the Same Time

### 1. Having and Doing

I have been much influenced by Alain de Botton's argument, in *The Pleasures and Sorrows of Work*, that Capitalism has not yet addressed our higher needs – but could and should. The final chapter of his book *The Architecture of Happiness* examines the tantalizing relationship between money, taste and beauty.

Instructions on how to sell your soul are thrillingly spelled out by Balzac in *Lost Illusions* (although be patient, the first part of this novel is much less exciting than the second) and its sequel, *The Splendour and Misery of Courtesans*.

## 2. What Rex Got Wrong and Other Lessons

The 1981 television adaptation of *Brideshead Revisited* brilliantly visualizes the scene in the restaurant. For information about the Landmark Trust see www.landmarktrust.org.uk.

# VII. My Place in the Big Picture

## 1. The Problems of the Rich

*The Rise of the Nouveaux Riches*, by architectural historian J. Mordaunt-Crook, is a fascinating study of the conflict between wealth and status in Britain during the second half of the nineteenth century. It traces the initial refusal of the existing aristocratic elite to mix socially with those who had recently made large fortunes and the gradual absorption of new wealth into the existing order.

The duties that fall to the rich are explored in Benjamin Disraeli's *Sybil* (1845) – still a very readable novel. *Sybil* has the subtitle 'The Two Nations', by which Disraeli means the rich and the poor. Disraeli did not advocate equality; he believed that the rich should justify their material advantages by providing true moral leadership for the whole of society, and he is very stern in his condemnation when they fail to live up to this noble role. *Sybil* is the single most remarkable work ever written by a British Prime Minister.

In *The Life You Can Save*, Peter Singer makes a trenchant argument that we owe immense moral responsibility to everyone in dire need. It is designed to induce massive guilt in the consciences of the rich.

## 2. *The Virtues of Poverty*

*The Mirror of Perfection* is a compilation of stories, dating from the fourteenth century, relating events from the life of St Francis of Assisi. It takes us inside the belief that voluntary poverty is the ideal human state.

## 3. *The Intimate Relationship with Money*

Balzac describes a miser's delight in contemplating his wealth in *Old Goriot*.

In his best novel – *Wilhelm Meister's Apprenticeship* – Goethe traces the evolution of Wilhelm's attitudes to money. At first Wilhelm despises commerce, but later he comes to have a very healthy respect for money as a necessary ingredient in making good things happen in the world. Finally he gets involved with a powerful group of social reformers who aim to change the world by good commercial management. Although written at the very end of the eighteenth century, the underlying themes are powerfully relevant today. In part six of my book *Love, Life, Goethe*, I discuss these ideas in more detail.

# Picture Acknowledgements

The author and publisher would like to thank the following for permission to reproduce the images used in this book:

Pages 12, 17, 72 and 93 Reproduced courtesy of Julian Scheffer

Page 16 *Moon Rising Over the Sea*, 1822, by Caspar David Friedrich (1774–1840) © Nationalgalerie, Berlin / The Bridgeman Art Library

Page 61 Well Walk © Roberto Herrett / Alamy

Pages 86–7 *The Artist's Brothers*, c.1830, by Wilhelm Ferdinand Bendz (1804–1832) © Den Hirschsprungske Samling / akg-images

Page 109 Antique shop © Wildscape / Alamy

Page 113 Royal Crescent © David Lyons / Alamy

Pages 126–7 The blue and silver dining room at 5 Belgrave Square, London designed by Stephane Boudin. Photograph © A.E.Henson / Country Life Picture Library

Pages 128–9 Mentmore Towers © Robert Stainforth / Alamy

Page 131 The Radcliffe Camera © naglestock.com / Alamy

Page 139 *Goethe in His Study Dictating to His Secretary John*, 1831, by Johann Joseph Schmeller (1796–1841) © Stiftung Weimarer Klassik /akg-images

Illustrations and diagrams on pages 11, 44, 49, 52 and 104 © Joana Niemeyer 2011

All other images provided courtesy of the author.

Notes

Notes

If you enjoyed this book and want to read more about life's big issues, you can find out about the series, buy books and get access to exclusive content at www.panmacmillan.com/theschooloflife

If you'd like to explore ideas for everyday living, THE SCHOOL OF LIFE runs a regular programme of classes, weekends, secular sermons and events in London and other cities around the world. Browse our shop and visit www.theschooloflife.com

**How to Thrive in the Digital Age**
Tom Chatfield

**How to Think More about Sex**
Alain de Botton

**How to Change the World**
John-Paul Flintoff

**How to Worry Less about Money**
John Armstrong

**How to Stay Sane**
Philippa Perry

**How to Find Fulfilling Work**
Roman Krznaric